MAR 1 9 2019

M000236496

Queer Lessons for Churches on the Straight and Narrow

What All Christians Can Learn from LGBTQ Lives

Cody J. Sanders

© 2013, Cody J. Sanders

Published in the United States by Faithlab., Macon GA,

www.faithlab.com

ISBN 978-0-9895753-1-7

All rights reserved. Printed in the United States of America.

Scripture quotations are from the New Revised Standard Version Bible, copyright © 1989 National Council of the Churches of Christ in the United States of America. Used by permission. All rights reserved.

To my grandparents
Charles and Shirley Maddox,
Johnny and Jo Ann Sanders

"One of the most provocative, unsettling, and transforming experiences of reading the Gospel is following Jesus as he reframes questions posed to him in ways that bring what is unstated and urgent to life. Cody Sanders has taken this approach as his model in *Queer Lessons for Churches on the Straight and Narrow*. This book is not a rehashing of old arguments about including LGBT people into the church or another smart reading of the 'clobber' texts — those 7 or so passages used by conservative religious leaders to demonize queer people. Rather, this is a book that asks a refreshing new set of questions about how Queer lives can heal our spirit and our congregations. Sanders is a beautiful writer who balances a pastoral understanding with a provocative edginess that challenges all of us to go deeper. I highly recommend this book."

- Sharon Groves, Ph.D., Director of Religion and Faith Programs,
Human Rights Campaign

"Sanders has written a seminal work, a must-read for veterans of the Welcoming Movement. For communities just beginning this conversation it opens a new set of questions that will shape a more compassionate process toward inclusion in the 21st Century. But perhaps most powerfully, it is a clarion call to all LGBTQ Christians to step fully into the space of prophets to and teachers for the church in this moment of profound disruption and change."

- Rev. Robin Lunn, Executive Director,
Association of Welcoming & Affirming Baptists

"Cody Sanders has written a must-read book for any church or individual who yearns to engage in faithful community. Dealing with topics such as relationship, community, love, and forgiveness, Rev. Sanders brings his wisdom and integrity as a queer person of faith, a pastoral counselor and a scholar. The book offers an invitation to imagine larger and more profound questions as communities engage in dialogue about significant issues for us all. The book is illustrative of what can emerge when we take time to learn with one another about the complexity of sexuality, gender identity and sexual orientation, and church. I look forward to using this book in my classes in pastoral care."

- Joretta L. Marshall, Ph.D., Executive Vice President and Dean, Professor of Pastoral Theology and Pastoral Care and Counseling, Brite Divinity School, Fort Worth, TX

"How might we reinvigorate struggling congregations and denominations? How do we inspire deep personal faith commitments and strong ties to congregational life? How can we overcome isolation to create and sustain communities of life-sustaining mutual care? How can churches and Christians who've become comfortable hold onto the Gospel imperative to live as justice-seeking catalysts for social change? If you are asking questions like this, you'd do well to read this book.

Cody Sanders asks good questions. And, in encouraging churches to move away from suspicious scrutiny and toward a robust compassionate curiosity into the lives of queer people, he suggests an intriguing, unexpected and life-giving place to find the answers.

In a scholarly and approachable manner, Sanders speaks in helpful ways to churches across the theological spectrum. Churches and denominations still in the midst of theological struggle on issues of sexuality will find practical ideas for shaping their questions and embodying faithful, loving community even as they continue their processes of discernment. Those that have declared themselves to be welcoming and those that have lived into that reality for years will find ways of going deeper and of using the lessons they've learned to recognize and address patterns of violence and injustice in all the places they appear. Those that have devoted themselves to working against other oppressions such as sexism, racism, and classism will hear a call to a fuller understanding of the interconnected nature of oppressions. These practices and ways of understanding that Sanders presents will continue to serve the church and its people well since, as he convincingly argues, 'Justice has no final frontier.'

Read this book and you'll come away with fresh, deep and restorative ways of thinking about relationships, community, faithfulness, love, violence, and forgiveness. This work demonstrates convincingly that all Christians and all congregations indeed have a great deal to learn from LGBTQ lives."

- Rev. LeDayne McLeese Polaski, Program Coordinator,
Baptist Peace Fellowship of North America

"*Queer Lessons for Churches on the Straight and Narrow* decisively changes the terms of conversation between LGBTQ people and church communities. In one deft volume full of grace and wisdom, Sanders enfranchises LGBTQ people as important resources with much to teach the very churches that historically marginalized them.

Instead of fruitless debates between predominantly heterosexual churches and gay people, many of whom have been faithful members of these churches for generations, Sanders lifts up the lessons of forgiveness, relationship, spirituality, and community that LGBTQ people have to teach contemporary faith communities. Without rancor or antagonism, yet unsparing in his critique of beliefs and behaviors of churches that have negatively impacted the LGBTQ community, Sanders guides readers of good will to new insights about faithful love and covenanted relationships in often hostile circumstances—practical, life-tested strategies that Christian communities can use to benefit all their members, straight and gay alike, here and now.

Sanders' ideas are refreshing and creative. *Queer Lessons* opens up new avenues of dialogue and shared experience between intelligent, loving, and devout people—offering everyone a chance to get on the same side for the real quest faith communities face in our increasingly polarized and politicized world: How to draw on the practical wisdom of a people who have so much to teach about flourishing in a negligent, difficult, and sometimes violent culture. *Queer Lessons for Churches on the Straight and Narrow* belongs on the bookshelves of laity and clergy alike, because it breaks new ground for everyone who loves "The Old, Old Story" of Jesus and the Good News.

You are going to love this book for its perceptive account of human nature, its daring thesis, and its unabashed, positive spirit. *Queer Lesson for Churches on the Straight and Narrow* is an instant classic in the field of church studies."

- Stephen V. Sprinkle, Ph.D., Director of Field Education and Supervised Ministry, Director of Baptist Studies, and Professor of Practical Theology at Brite Divinity School, Fort Worth, Texas, and Theologian-in-Residence at Cathedral of Hope United Church of Christ, Dallas, Texas.

"Cody Sanders reminds us in *Queer Lessons* that Jesus' ministry was a queerying one. In order to help us live new lives centered in the gospel, Jesus asked new and different questions. And so does Sanders. The answers turn our relationship with LGBTQ lives on its head. That which has been reviled, dangerous or to be protected against becomes a source of wisdom, love and faithfulness. 'The stone that the builders rejected has become the cornerstone' takes on a new meaning through Sanders' work. I am grateful and know you will be, too!"

- Rev. Dr. Rebecca Voelkel, Program Director, Institute for Welcoming Resources, National Gay and Lesbian Task Force

"What urgent new (smart) questions must Christians ask when they finally quit asking those tired old (stupid) questions about Queer people? And why are Queer people best prepared to answer them? Read Cody Sanders' inspired first book *Queer Lessons for Churches on the Straight and Narrow*. The Preface alone — explaining the term 'Queer' — makes it a 'must-read' for everyone concerned about the future of the Christian church, Queer and Straight alike."

- Rev. Dr. Mel White, Co-founder of Soulforce and author of
Stranger at the Gate: To Be Gay and Christian in America

Contents

Acknowledgements

In April of 2012 at a conference organized by the Cooperative Baptist Fellowship and Mercer University titled "A [Baptist] Conference on Sexuality and Covenant," I delivered a plenary address posing the question: *What can churches learn about "covenant" from the example of same-sex relationships?* About two months after this conference, I met Jim Dant, editor at FaithLab, who was in attendance at the April conference in Decatur, Georgia. It was Jim who first posed to me the idea of writing this book and expressed his enthusiastic commitment to seeing it published by FaithLab. I am very thankful for this prompting.

As I prepared the manuscript, Angela Yarber and Darnell Moore read select chapters and provided helpful comments from their perspectives as faithfully-engaged scholar-activists. Chet Andrews also read chapters and engaged in dialogue with me on the framework of the book, helping me see the benefits and limitations of the text for churches not yet openly affirming of LGBTQ people.

My friend and ministerial colleague, Sam Coates, diligently read the entire manuscript, chapter by chapter, providing helpful critique and suggestions regarding the book's usefulness for congregations wishing to learn from the lives of LGBTQ people.

Stephen V. Sprinkle, a friend and mentor in the work of justice-seeking for LGBTQ lives, provided valuable advice to me at the outset of this project, for which I am grateful.

I must also acknowledge the role my mentor and teacher, Joretta L. Marshall, has played in the background of this book. Joretta continually instills in me the value of asking good questions.

Finally, my partner, Ben Curry, is always my first and most patient editor, enduring my vacillations between satisfaction and despair over the worthwhileness of my writing. The book is vastly better than it would otherwise be without his careful attention to and endless conversation about the book's content.

These collaborators should all be credited with helping to bring clarity to the ideas presented here, but should not be held responsible for the errors and complications they undoubtedly attempted to correct.

Preface

Why *Queer?*

"Queer" is a word we all know, but few of us use it. "Queer" is a word with life. You can't hear it without an emotional — even visceral — response. The word *does* something to you. It acts upon you.

If you were the kid in the middle school hallways who felt the force of the word through the velocity of a bully's blows, hearing it may still cause your stomach to churn. Queer means blood and bruises and tears and fear. Maybe you've had enough of hearing it.

If you were the bully whose lips became practiced at forming the word whenever you stood within shouting distance of those "little queers," it means something different. It may mean shame and regret for the vitriol you spewed forth in torment of your peers. You may wish you could just forget the word altogether, to disavow its place in the lexicon of the vernacular.

Some have neither of these associations, but still find the word unbecoming. It's just not a *nice* word, too undignified for respectable conversation, sullied by questionable associations.

Sometimes queer is used as simple shorthand, cutting down on the cumbersome acronyms of the sexual/gender alphabet soup (e.g., LGBTTQQIAA — lesbian, gay, bisexual, transgender, two-spirit, queer, questioning, intersex, asexual, ally . . . more could be added).[1] Queer becomes a term of unification, bringing together everyone experiencing injustice and violence based on their sexuality or gender identity beneath one tiny term. But its power transcends that of mere linguistic convenience.

Queer is a word of remembrance. Like many terms of derision employed as rhetorical weapons against minority groups, queer continually takes on new life. Because we (queers) can't let you forget. And we, too, must be prompted to remember.

When *we* use the term — that is, when spoken by those of us who identify as somehow queer in our sexuality or gender identity — we are claiming a term once (and often still) used to enact violence against us, and reappropriating it as a term of unity and defiant pride. It is a movement of strength and resolve that says, "We won't let you forever own this word as a term of contempt."

But it is also a rhetorical trick we play so that none may forget. Forgetting is too easy an escape. Even as a reappropriated term of pride, queer forces all to remember its cruel etymological past. It says something about who we think we are and aspire to become. And, in the same breath, what we've seen, what we've experienced, what we've done and what's been done to us, and what we refuse to allow any longer.

Queer is a word of resistance. Even as it is employed as a shorthand term of wide inclusion, queer calls our attention to the limitation on our linguistic capacity to define others. Queer stands in resistance to our definitional capacity and our presumed power to name and know "others." It challenges the binary terms we use to categorize human being and experience with words like straight/gay and male/female. Where our medical, psychiatric, and religious ways of speaking about gender and sexuality provide us with these linguistic categories and attach to them valuations of the healthy/unhealthy, normal/pathological, holy/profane — queer stands in disruption. Queer scholarship disrupts the seeming naturalness of our categorizations by lifting the veil on their histories and it disturbs their supposed innocence by implicating their attachments to power — the power to define what is true, real, and good in life and experience.[2]

While I use the word "queer" as a term of inclusion to encompass persons who live against the grain of heterosexual norms and biological gender conformity — people we might refer to with terms like "lesbian," "gay," "bisexual," "transgender," "sexually questioning," "intersex," "asexual," etc. — I also hope you will feel the word packing a little more punch than a simple term of all-encompassing convenience.

Even when used as a term of unification for numerous sexual and gender identifications, queer must simultaneously represent a resistance to the erasure of these diverse identifications — as if one word could encompass the rich differences that shape our lives. Rather than a simple unity of identifiers, queer represents the multiplicity of each individual's identities. Rather than a static understanding of our sense of self, queer should remind us of the continued flux of identities in which each of us lives. Rather than an identity, queer should remind us of the complexity of all of our identities, claiming that there is more to our sense of identity than can be captured by either the terms of identification applied to us and those that are self-chosen by us.

Queer should disturb us, shake us up a bit, skew our perception. Just when you think you've "got it," experience the queer trickery being played upon your conceptual grasp causing you to return to the questions you once felt sure you had answered. Queer calls us to question commonsensical knowledge and perspectives, to form, *re*form, and *de*form our knowledge of sexual and gender difference.

Queer is a word of unification of those targeted by prejudice and injustice. It is a word of remembrance spoken to those who wish to forget the word and all of the lives it has marked. Queer is a term of resistance to the easy ways we categorize others based upon our perceptions of human difference. And queer is a word of invitation to move beyond — beyond practices of division and devaluation of human life, beyond overly simple categories for understanding human difference, and beyond the limited set of questions that we are typically found asking about queer lives.

Notes

[1]Readers encountering the diversity of terminology surrounding sexuality and gender identity for the first time might benefit from a further brief explanation of a few of these terms. While **sexual orientation** refers to one's primary attractions and desires for physical, sexual, spiritual, or emotional intimacy, **gender identity** is used in reference to one's social, psychological, spiritual, and behavioral experience and expression of gender as male or female, both, neither, or those for whom gender is experienced in a more fluid state not captured by the male/female binary.

With regard to sexual orientation, while the term **homosexual** was once commonly in use among those affirming of gays and lesbians, today this term is typically heard with a cold, clinical ring and is used most widely among those holding a non-affirming stance in relation to same-sex attracted persons. Presently, it is rarely used as a term of self-description among gays and lesbians. Today, it is far more common to hear men whose emotional, physical and sexual attraction is toward other men referred to as **gay**, women attracted to women referred to as **lesbian**, and men and women who experience attraction to both men and women referred to as **bisexual**. In many African American contexts, the term **same-gender-loving** (SGL) is preferred to the terms gay, lesbian, or queer.

The term **transgender** is used in reference to persons whose own psychological and spiritual sense of gender differs from the social and cultural expectations attached to the biological/physical sex characteristics with which they were born. **Transsexual** is often used to refer to those who experience a desire to change bodily characteristics through surgical or hormonal treatments in order to achieve a closer match between bodily appearance and psychological/spiritual gender identity. **Intersex** is a term used to denote persons whose physical, hormonal, or chromosomal sex characteristics at birth do not fit neatly into the categories of either male or female. And, finally, **gender queer** is sometimes used by those whose internal sense and external expression of gender transgresses binary categorizations like male and female.

The acronym **LGBT** or **LGBTQ** is commonly used to denote lesbian, gay, bisexual, transgender and queer or questioning people.

[2] This usage of queer is most akin to that employed in queer theory and queer theology. For further exploration of these fields of inquiry, see Annamarie Jagose, *Queer Theory: An Introduction* (Washington Square, NY: New York University Press, 1996).

Introduction

Changing the Questions

Debates are raging over queer lives in both churches and the political sphere. These debates usually produce two, very polarized sides representing seemingly irreconcilable perspectives. But what if we were able to start the conversation over? Imagine if the entire conversation about queer lives and Christian faith had its start in your living room or your own local congregation. If you could ask the first question to a group of interested and engaged conversation partners, what would it be? Would you accept the terms of the current debates, or would you choose a new starting place? How would you keep the conversation from devolving into an overly simplified and polarized argument?

While there is no starting over, this book is about imagining new pathways into old conversations. It is an invitation to question the terms of the debates into which we've been drawn. It is a book less concerned with answering questions and, instead, aims toward cultivating the imagination necessary to ask new questions. And new questions about queer lives and Christian faith couldn't come at a more appropriate time.

Between Invisible and Everywhere: "Learn from Us"

We stand at a critical juncture in time for the navigation of relationships between queer people and faith communities. We occupy a transitional space of great possibility — a threshold between the already and the not yet, the well-established past and the now-inaugurated future.

On one side of our contemporary setting is a long era of queer invisibility. During this era, queer people were kept out of sight in everyday life. Forces of law, medicine, and religion worked to keep queer people hidden through the criminalization of homosexuality with sodomy laws and police raids, the pathologizing of homosexuality as an illness, and the stigmatization of homosexuality as a nearly unspeakable sin.[1]

Gay rights historian, John D'Emilio, describes the efforts of gays and lesbians to emerge from this era of queer invisibility during the early days of the gay rights movement in the United States. He encapsulates the objectives of gays and lesbians in the early days of the gay rights or gay liberation movement with phrases to summarize the efforts of each era of the movement. A look at this recent history reveals a steady trajectory away from a lengthy period of queer invisibility.

In the post-World War II era, McCarthyism aimed not only to quell a presumed Communist tide, but the U.S. government also expended great effort to investigate "sex perverts" — conducting investigations on gays and lesbians, instituting the surveillance of gay community gatherings, and opening the mail of suspected homosexuals.[2] D'Emilio encapsulates the outlook and strategic approach of gay movements that emerged during this era with the phrase, "give us a hearing."[3] Throughout the 1950s and into the 1960s, gays and lesbians worked to gain this hearing — in their own words and on their own terms — by publishing material on homosexuality and initiating dialogue with professionals in medicine, law, and the church in order to counter the negative views of gays and lesbians that prevailed in society.

In the 1970s and early 1980s, D'Emilio defines the character of the movement toward gay rights with the phrase, "here we are."[4] Inspired and propelled by the energy of the civil rights movement of the 1960s, queer people began making their presence in U.S. society widely known. In defiance of previous efforts to make queer people invisible, movements toward justice began to shape gay and lesbian organizations and community groups, placing a prime importance on gay and lesbian individuals becoming visible through the act of "coming out" to publicly and proudly claim their identification as gay or lesbian.

In the next era, "leave us alone" typified the attitude of many gays and lesbians who worked toward the elimination of sodomy laws, the removal of homosexuality as a psychiatric disorder, the lessening of police harassment, and the institution of discrimination protections for gays and lesbians. D'Emilio describes the message of gays and lesbians in this era with two additional phrases: "Get out of our bedrooms and out of our psyches" and "Put a stop to our mistreatment."[5] With increasing visibility and better organization, queer people sought space to live their lives without judgmental intrusion, discrimination, and harassment.

In the early 1990s, gay organizations began to work in earnest toward a new set of goals for recognition and inclusion. During this era, queer people sought the legal recognition of same-sex relationships, rights for gay and lesbian parents, the founding of gay-straight alliance organizations, and safer schools for queer students. D'Emilio encapsulates this effort with the phrase, "we want in" — an era of increasing rights for a now very-visible queer people.[6]

It is an impressive movement from a pleading, "*give us a hearing*," to a defiant, "*here we are*," to a fed up, "*leave us alone*," to an entitled, "*we want in.*" While never a monolithic, single-minded movement, the progress queer people in the United States have made from World War II to the present is evidence of a progressive movement out of a legally-, medically-, and religiously-enforced invisibility. Defying those who would criminalize, demonize, and pathologize us, queer people gradually laid hold of the rights and protections we believed to belong to us.

And now a new era is upon us. Just on the horizon of our contemporary setting is an almost-here era of queer ubiquity. This is a time already present for many whose lives are increasingly populated with queer people. But no matter your social setting, your congregational make-up, or your circle of friends — queer people are everywhere. There are queer politicians, queer public figures, and queer journalists.[7] At the outset of 2013, same-sex couples can enjoy the rights, benefits and protections of legal marriage in thirteen states and D.C. Queer people can openly serve in the U.S. military and enjoy the protection of a federal hate crimes prevention act.[8] More churches and denominations than ever are ordaining lesbian, gay, bisexual, and transgender clergy and blessing our marriages and unions.

In our media saturated society, perhaps the strongest evidence of an emerging queer ubiquity is the presence of lesbian, gay, bisexual, and transgender characters playing central roles in primetime, family-oriented programming on nearly every major television network.[9] Ubiquity: queer people are everywhere and are becoming so commonplace, so ordinary, that it isn't too fanciful to imagine that, before long, little attention will be given to sexual orientation and gender identity as controversial or provocative markers of human difference.

And here we are, in-between, moving closer to the later era of queer ubiquity, but still influenced by the oppressive forces driving the former era of invisibility. After all, as many gains as queer people have made from enforced invisibility toward greater visibility, legal rights and social equality, we continue to live amid a great deal of queer negativity. While many states institute same-sex marriage, others pass propositions to shore up the definition of marriage between a man and a woman. As many churches open their doors and pathways to ordination for queer people,[10] many others become virulently hostile to an increasingly visible population of queer people in their communities. It is premature to claim that the era of queer ubiquity has fully arrived, even as it seems almost inevitably on its way.

In the emerging era of queer ubiquity in which queer people will become so commonplace as to be boring topics of conversation, we can look forward to some important gains, as well as some critical losses. Queer ubiquity might mean that we no longer debate the place of queer people in society — ceasing to haggle over their rights and scoff at their expectations to be protected from discrimination and violence. Queer people will enjoy the rights, privileges, and protections of heterosexual people within our democracy. Able to legally marry our same-sex partners, adopt and parent children, speak openly about our sexuality and our queer loved ones without fear of violence and workplace discrimination, and able to grow up in the safety of schools that do not punish and pathologize queer youth, we stand to gain a great deal by becoming commonplace, ordinary, and boring topics of conversation. In this future era, the presence of queer people might be encapsulated by the phrase, "We're just like you."

But in an era in which queer people are "just like you" — ubiquitous, ordinary, and commonplace — we may also be faced with a few significant losses, making our current situation a critical moment of in-between space. Following D'Emilio's lead to encapsulate the need of our current critical juncture in time with a pithy phrase, I might suggest this one: "Learn from us." Before its too late, learn from us. While we are still asking questions about sexual orientation and gender identity as critical markers of human difference, let us begin asking more interesting and important questions about queer lives. With an era of queer ubiquity still on the horizon — not yet fully present but surely on its way — churches have the opportunity to learn from the lives of queer people. Now — while the subject of queer lives is still interesting, provocative, and controversial — we have the opportunity to engage this interest and controversy in our churches by shedding our worn-out strategies of suspicion toward queer people, changing the questions we choose to ask about queer lives, and engaging in a compassionate curiosity that invites us all to learn from queer lives — before we become too boring to talk about any longer.

Shedding Our Worn-Out Strategies

It matters which questions we choose to ask, and for a long time now, churches have been asking a very limited set of questions about sexuality. Nearly every denomination in the United States — from the most "conservative" to the most "liberal" — is asking some kinds of questions about sexuality. Some of these questions stem from changing tides within denominations about same-sex sexual orientations. These churches are finding the need to ask questions about what forms "inclusion" and "affirmation" of queer people should take around church membership, ordination, and marriage. In other contexts, the questions emerge from a reactionary posture addressing a changing cultural attitude toward sexual orientation and gender identity. These churches can be found asking questions about who is "in" and who is "out" of Christian fellowship. Still others are asking questions of genuine curiosity about sexual orientation and gender identity; confronted with new realities they aren't yet prepared to address through the lens of faith.

Our traditional strategy for these questions has been one of suspicious scrutiny. Churches have long been suspicious toward forms of human difference. Whether race, gender, class, gender identity, sexual orientation, or religious affiliation, churches have perfected a suspicious gaze toward those who differ from the social or congregational norm. These suspicious questions typically go something like this: Can someone be both gay and a faithful Christian? How should congregations respond to gay people? Should we allow gays and lesbians access to church membership, leadership positions, or ordination if they are involved in same-sex relationships? Are gay people excluded from the covenant of marriage based on their same-gender-loving status?

The strategy of suspicious scrutiny produces a set of questions that assume a particular arrangement of power. Each of these questions presumes a position of inclusion and another of exclusion — inside/ outside, center/margin. Those in positions of privilege by virtue of their heterosexual or gender-conforming identification get to do all the asking. And the questions asked assume the askers occupy a stable center —

in this case, a center in which heterosexuality is the presumed norm — and that there are strange *others* on the margins trying to get "in." Beneath the surface, the questions are about maintaining certain boundaries — boundaries of Christian faithfulness, of church membership, of ordination to the clergy, of the covenantal bond and legal contract of marriage.

A posture of suspicious scrutiny leads to many ways of investigating the questions we ask about queer people. Sometimes we turn to the scriptures and ask, "What does the Bible say about homosexuality?" Others turn to historical precedent and ask, "Can it be any other way?" Scientific sources are another avenue by which we inquire, "How did they get that way — by choice or by nature?" All of these strategies continue to avert our gaze away from the lived human realities of the "subjects" of inquiry and, instead, bolster our suspicion with sources that can be used to talk about those subjects.

These limited questions are evidence of a worn-out strategy. Not only are these questions limited in their scope, they are also limiting in their ability to carry our churches into a meaningful future. This claim may seem too strong at first. But the questions we ask really do matter that much. Questions formed out of suspicion toward human difference do produce certain results, but these outcomes typically take the shape of boundary maintenance. For example: Can someone be both gay and a faithful Christian? If the answer arrived upon is "no," then shore up the boundaries of church membership, ordination, Christian marriage, etc. Keep those who don't fit the norm "out." If "yes," then shift the boundaries outward a bit to include more people in these institutions. Let some of *them* "in." If we're still unsure, then let's just agree that these are the boundaries we have for now — probably for good reason — and if they need to change, someone else will have to change them.

No matter how you answer the questions, the strategy of suspicious scrutiny is tepid, ineffectual, and unendingly frustrating. As a queer person, I have grown tired of talking about sexuality — and my own life — on other people's terms. It is exhausting to answer the same old set of questions again and again. And it becomes utterly infuriating when you realize that the same people are asking these same questions relentlessly with seemingly little interest in any response that contradicts what they already "know" about the subject.

The strategy of many congregations is simply to change the subject in order to avoid questions of sexuality altogether. The only option for many queer people is to get as far away from the suspicious gaze of churches as possible — and often for good reason, after living their lives in ecclesiastical petri dishes, subjected to the poking and prodding of suspicious scrutiny. And no matter the outcome of the inquiry, all are left with some sore spots, hurt feelings, and broken relationships because the questions themselves construct a situation with little room for anything more than a "right" answer and a "wrong" answer with attendant justifications. Some come out on the "winning" side and others "lose."

It's not that questions of inclusion aren't important. As noted above, many lesbian, gay, bisexual, transgender, and straight people have worked diligently to increase the inclusivity of Christian churches and denominations, as well as society at large. These inclusive spaces provide breathing room for those who desire to practice their faith without scrutiny, follow their callings without hindrance, wed their partners with joy, and live their lives in safety. The questions that lead us to inclusion are, indeed, important. It is largely because these questions of inclusion have been so steadily answered by congregations responding with welcome and affirmation for queer people that we can now consider a new range of questions. But we simply cannot rest satisfied when we have settled the questions of inclusion because, in the end, they are unimaginative questions with very little life beyond the answer. They don't move our hearts, only our boundaries. They don't provoke our theological imagination, only the rearrangement of our theological beliefs. Too often, they fail to get us moving in creative directions, but only serve to get us stuck in a morass of conflicting views. It is time for churches to ask new questions.

Changing the Questions, Not the Subject

My proudest moments as a therapist are the ones when I am able to ask well-crafted questions. When it becomes obvious that a client and I become stuck — arriving at an impasse and not quite certain how to proceed — I often wonder to myself, "What question might get us moving again?" A good question has that ability. Questions can move us in ways that propositions and statements and truths and speculations cannot. A question, carefully crafted and presented at just the right moment, opens space for dialogue and discovery. Questions create room to move — not the movement of liner progression toward the "right" answer, but room to explore, to grow, to become genuinely curious.

As churches continue to form questions about human difference evidenced in sexual orientation and gender identity, we would do well to spend generous time and creative energy carefully cultivating the questions we choose to ask. We must ask ourselves what possibilities are opened to us by the questions we ask. Are our questions formed out of anxiety and fear? Or, do they express genuine curiosity and a willingness to explore? Do our questions presume that there are boundaries to be maintained and position us as the guardians of the status quo? Or, do our questions provoke thoughtful consideration and hold the potential to generate new perspectives, new insight, and even new questions?

In our quest to ask better questions, we need only look to the central figure of the Christian faith for inspiration. Jesus was a master at crafting beautiful questions. He asked questions that surprised, questions that infuriated, and questions that spurned the status quo lines of inquiry, leading people to ask to different, more important questions.

A helpful exercise for churches would be to re-read the four gospels, paying specific attention to each time the gospel writers place a question upon the lips of Jesus. Some of these questions may come to surprise us when we set aside the lesson we believe the text is teaching and carefully attend to how these questions are used in the narrative. A few examples may suffice to illustrate how re-reading the questions of

Jesus may invigorate our theological imaginations concerning the place of well-formed, provocative questions in the life of faith.

The third chapter of Mark's gospel begins and ends with the provocative questions of Jesus. At the chapter's outset (vv. 1-6), Jesus is pictured teaching in the synagogue on the Sabbath. Jesus finds himself in the presence of a man with a withered right hand and a crowd looking on him with suspicion, waiting to see if he would transgress the law to heal on the Sabbath. Rather than delivering a lesson on the meaning of the Sabbath or the merits of a healing act or simply healing the man and waiting for the crowd's reaction, Jesus prefaces the healing with a question for the suspicious onlookers: "Is it lawful to do good or to do harm on the sabbath, to save life or to kill?" (v. 4).

The question itself didn't simply settle the matter, as many were still angered by his act of healing on the Sabbath. But the query subverted the initial question lingering in the minds of the onlookers, i.e. "Should Jesus heal this man on the Sabbath?" which required a simple "yes" or "no" response. Instead, the question invited a more complex reflection on the law's relation to doing good, doing harm, appropriate observance of the Sabbath, and the demonstration of compassion.

At the end of the chapter (vv. 31-35), Jesus is again pictured in the midst of a crowd. In search of him, his mother and brothers sent someone into the crowd to retrieve Jesus. The messenger related to Jesus that his mother and brothers were waiting for him outside. In the presence of those gathered, Jesus asked the messenger an astounding question: "Who are my mother and my brothers?" (v. 33). Here, Jesus asks a simple question — one that everyone could presumably answer with ease and clarity. Yet, Jesus uses this confounding interrogative to invite his hearers to consider an expanded view of relatedness and family, later adding, "Whoever does the will of God is my brother and sister and mother" (v. 35).

Putting aside for the moment any theological meaning that might be made of these texts, the questions themselves point to the power of a question to open space for movement in dialogue and exploration.

They illustrate the beauty with which Jesus was able to place questions into the midst of anxious situations in order to subvert the black-and-white, right-or-wrong mentality held by many of his hearers. Yet, as illustrated by the first passage above, simply asking a different question doesn't always lessen the degree of difficulty or discomfort experienced by those who are invited into more complex exploration and inquiry. New questions, as helpful as they may be, often lead to the learning of difficult lessons.

Learning to Learn Queer Lessons

Queer lessons may be difficult for churches to learn. They are lessons we aren't used to learning from those we too often purport to teach. Indeed, churches have been trying to "teach" queer people for far too long. And queer people have often ended up worse off for the lessons we've been asked to learn.

Churches have often endeavored to teach us how to "straighten up," so to speak. They've produced countless sermons, programs, and ad campaigns designed to "teach us" about our sinfulness. Ex-gay ministries have endeavored to "teach us" the reasons we are who we are and show us a way out of our "homosexual lifestyle." These "lessons" have been cruel, unhelpful and most often a source of psychological and spiritual violence against queer souls. It is now time for churches to shift from their positions as teachers of (often unwilling) queer pupils to attentive students of queer lives.

Learning to learn queer lessons can be a disturbing process for churches. Learning to learn from queer lives invites us to change our positions in the conversation. An attitude of suspicious scrutiny allows those in the center of privilege, inclusion, and power (i.e., heterosexual and gender-conforming people) to ask all of the questions about those on the margins — interrogating our lives and our loves with a skeptical gaze. Those in positions of privilege set the terms of the conversation, decide which questions they will ask and even which responses they are willing to hear.

In contrast, we are invited into a process of "learning to learn from below."[11] We must learn to learn again, this time from those who have been oppressed, hidden, and silenced by the teachings of those in positions of sexual and gender privilege. Our old, worn-out strategies of suspicious scrutiny are so ingrained in our mentality that the process is not as simple as learning new lessons. It must, instead, be a much more gradual and intentional process of changing our churches' position in the conversation on sexuality and gender identity — a process of learning to learn again with fresh questions and new teachers.

By no means are queer people the only marginalized people from whom churches should learn lessons about life and Christian faith. Any group forced to exist for any length of time at the margins of church and society has much to teach those in privileged, majority-culture positions. Queer theologian Elizabeth Stuart argues, "The space of the marginalized is often a space where imagination can flourish outside the restricting dictates of the mainstream."[12] But this book is about queer lives and the lessons churches may learn from queer people, one group from which churches seem especially resistant to learning.

Some of these queer lessons we may learn by looking carefully, attentively, and appreciatively at the lives of lesbian, gay, bisexual, and transgender persons who have — for too long — been forcefully kept at the margins of church and society. We must ask, "What practices of relationship, what configurations of community, and forms of religious faithfulness have become life-enhancing — even salvific — as queer people were marginalized by the majority in church and society?" This is the aim of chapters one, two, and three.

Other queer lessons will come as instruction derived from the examination of the intersections between queer lives and the Christian tradition. At these intersections, we can examine churches' varied deal-ings with human difference, asking, "How have the lives of queer people intersected with churches and the Christian tradition in ways that teach us something about broad, important themes like love, violence, and forgiveness?" This is the aim of chapters four, five, and six.

Churches On the "Straight and Narrow"

This book is intended for several audiences. It aims to provide another way forward for churches in which "straight" (i.e., heterosexual) is the privileged norm, and the line of questioning about sexual and gender difference is "narrow" in its focus upon suspicious questions of inclusion/exclusion and boundary maintenance. The straight and narrow line of inquiry transcends denominational lines and divisions of conservative or liberal. The presumption of a straight, heterosexual norm and narrow lines of suspicious inquiry are typical of many church contexts, even churches that come to positions of welcome and affirmation of queer people. Indeed, even welcoming and affirming churches do not often move beyond a strategy in which questions of inclusion/exclusion have led otherwise straight norms to accommodate queer people — falling far short of actually learning from queer lives. Beyond this straight and narrow path, this book aims to open space for churches willing to learn to learn from queer lives, willing to ask an important new set of questions, and willing to be changed by the process.

Some individuals and churches will find this book helpful when the old methods of suspicious scrutiny feel worn out. This shouldn't be seen as a more advanced book, in that you need to have read other books and encountered other information on sexuality and faith before making use of this one. Rather, this should be seen as a book with a different approach to questions about sexuality and Christian faith — a book asking different questions about the same subject. So if you're starting your reading on the subject of sexuality and gender identity with this book, read on. Or, if you've found other approaches to the subject stifling and leading dialogue to dead ends, I hope this book can help to create some new conversational movement through asking different questions.

Other individuals and congregations, having been welcoming and affirming of queer people for some time, may find this book helpful in fueling movement to a new stage of dialogue on sexuality and faith. Even welcoming and affirming congregations may find themselves on the straight and narrow when it comes to the questions they ask and the strategies of inquiry they employ. Often, the questions congregations ask in order to arrive at a place of welcome and affirmation of queer people aren't that different from the questions asked by non-affirming congregations. The answers are just different. So even if your questions have led to greater inclusion and affirmation for queer people in your congregation, I hope this book can provide avenues for a compassionate curiosity into the lives of those queer people you now affirm. Learning to learn from queer lives may lead to more meaningful change and more refreshing renewal than can be produced by a simple outward movement of the boundaries of inclusion.

A Note To Queer Readers

I write as an openly queer person, an ordained Baptist minister, and in a covenanted same-sex partnership with another queer Baptist minister. While I hope this book can be useful to churches seeking to ask better questions about sexuality and gender identity, I also hope that some queer readers will find this book helpful in developing new approaches to the communities of faith in which they are involved. I am aware that some queer people may see this book as an attempt to baptize queer "virtues" and Christianize queer people who have, for quite a long time, enacted a necessary resistance to all manner of violence visited upon queer bodies by "Christian" people. This is certainly not my intention and I hope that queer readers might find in this book a springboard for reworking the questions posed about us and reimagining the possibilities our queer lives hold for communities of faith.

If, however, I am to fault churches with a long history of asking a very limited and limiting set of questions about sexuality, I must also acknowledge that queer people have, for far too long, accepted the terms of the debate given to them by those who seek to oppose our lives and loves.[13] Some queer people have addressed the questions posed about them by producing an array of very helpful apologetic sources that seek to change minds about "what the Bible says" concerning homosexuality. Others accepted the terms of the debate and, quite understandably, needed to distance themselves from the sources of scrutiny that threatened to sap every ounce of emotional health and spiritual life from them. But whether we, as queer people, stay within our churches and work toward affirmation and reform or take our leave of church altogether, there remains a need to become more critical about the terms upon which churches' questions are posed.

I hope this book will be useful in sparking the creativity of our theological imaginations, helping churches to ask a new set of questions. There are certainly far too many queer lessons to be learned than any one of us can imagine on our own. Whatever position queer people may have held in churches through the years — hiding in plain sight, long-forgotten exiles, martyrs, oft-ignored prophets at the margins, steady reformers of the status quo — one mantle we might all become more accustomed to taking up is that of queer teacher. Long after queer people have achieved full equality in church and society, churches will continue to need the queer lessons our lives have to offer. We have much to teach.

Notes

[1] Even as these tools served to invisibalize queer people, they may also be seen as the primary means by which the "homosexual" was *produced* as a stable, encompassing "identity" category. The production of a homosexual "identity" is explored by Michel Foucault in *The History of Sexuality*, Vol. 1 (New York: Vintage Books, 1978).

[2] John D'Emilio, *The World Turned: Essays on Gay History, Politics, and Culture* (Durham, NC: Duke University Press, 2002), 80.

[3] D'Emilio, *The World Turned*, 94-5.

[4] D'Emilio, *The World Turned*, 95.

[5] D'Emilio, *The World Turned*, 96.

[6] D'Emilio, *The World Turned*, 97.

[7]In the 2012 U.S. election, Tammy Baldwin from Wisconsin became the first openly gay or lesbian person to win a seat in the U.S. Senate, joining a number of already openly gay and lesbian members of the U.S. House of Representatives, not to mention the myriad state and local politicians who identify as lesbian, gay, bisexual, transgender, or queer. For information on openly LGBTQ politicians, see the *Gay & Lesbian Victory Fund* at www.victoryfund.org.

[8]The U.S. policy prohibiting openly gay, lesbian, or bisexual persons from serving in the military called, "Don't ask, don't tell," was repealed by congress and the repeal was signed into law by President Obama on December 22, 2010. The Matthew Shepard and James Byrd, Jr. Hate Crimes Prevention Act was passed by Congress and signed into law by President Obama on October 28, 2009.

[9]As of the Fall 2012, there are gay leading characters on *Glee* (Fox), *The New Normal* (NBC), *Modern Family* (ABC).

[10]In 2003, Gene Robinson was elected the first openly gay bishop in the Episcopal Church in the United States of America. Today, many mainline denominations have opened pathways to ordination and clergy recognition for lesbian, gay, bisexual and transgender people, including the United Church of Christ in 1972, the Evangelical Lutheran Church of American in 2009, the Presbyterian Church (U.S.A.) in 2011, and my own denomination, the Alliance of Baptists.

[11]"Learning to learn from below" is a phrase attributable to the postcolonial theorist, Gayatri Chakravorty Spivak, used in describing one movement of her deconstructive postcolonial methodology. For an exploration of Spivak's method, see, Sangeeta Ray, "An Ethics on the Run," *PMLA* 123, no. 1 (2008).

[12]Elizabeth Stuart, *Just Good Friends: Towards a Lesbian and Gay Theology of Relationships* (New York: Mowbray, 1995), 5.

[13]While a cadre of scholars—queer theologians—have long surpassed the traditional terms of Christian sexuality debates in order to produce profound theological treatments of sexuality and Christian theology, these efforts have not often reached very far into the pews, where conversation on sexual orientation continues to be dominated by traditional terms of the debate. For an historical account of these queer theological endeavors, see Elizabeth Stuart, *Gay and Lesbian Theologies: Repetitions with Critical Difference* (Burlington, VT: Ashgate, 2003), and Patrick S. Cheng, *Radical Love: An Introduction to Queer Theology* (New York: Seabury, 2011).

Chapter One

Lessons on Relationship

With each election cycle we see the possibilities opening further and further for same-sex couples to form legal marital bonds. At the time of this writing, thirteen states and D.C. have legalized same-sex marriage, either through a legislative act, court rulings, or by vote of the citizenry. The question we have become accustomed to asking — "Should same-sex couples be allowed to legally marry?" — is steadily being answered in the affirmative.

The progress in the legalization of same-sex marriage represents significant gains toward equality for gay and lesbian couples wishing to enjoy the same rights, benefits, and protections under the law as their straight neighbors.[1] But churches have been far too consumed with questioning the legitimacy of same-sex relationships to wonder about how this supposed "shaking of the foundations of civilization" might just shake open enough room for us to reexamine Christian practices of covenanted relationship. Queer folks, for our part, have often been too frenzied with achieving the constant inch-by-inch movement toward the legalization of same-sex marriage to pursue other avenues of inquiry into the formation of relationships.[2]

But if we could reframe the issue at hand not around the "ever-crumbling foundations of marriage" — as many churches do — nor as the pinnacle achievement of civil rights equality with heterosexuals — as many queer groups do — how might this change the questions we ask? If we could appreciate the possibilities opened to us by the shifting nature of social, legal, and religious conceptions of marriage, rather than fear these changes, might we discover some potential for growth? If churches possessed a bit of wonderment, rather than dread, over the abilities of queer people to forge intimate partnerships and covenanted relationships despite decades and decades of nearly total opposition from every corner of society, we might find ourselves asking:

"What have queer people learned about the formation of relationships that we would all benefit from knowing?"

For a very long time now — even in climates that exclude legal and religious recognition of covenanted relationships for lesbian, gay, and bisexual persons — same-sex partners have continued to enter covenanted relationship with one another amidst legal delegitimation, religious disparagement, and social disdain. In an era when so many familial, community, church, and legal supports are provided for straight couples in forging strong marital bonds (that still don't work about half the time), churches should become increasingly curious about what lesbian and gay couples have learned about forming relationships at the margins of church, society, local communities, and often their own biological families that everyone (even churches) needs to discover. But our learning must extend far beyond the legal definition of marriage.

Marriage Equality: Necessary But Not Enough

You don't need to believe in the legitimacy of gay marriage to understand why many queer people find marriage equality a necessary legal and political battle to wage. Though many churches and preachers have come to enjoy entering public discussions on the "definition of marriage," these sermons often cast "marriage" in the theological abstract, giving little recognition to the ways "marriage" has also become a legal category of relationship that carries with it rights, benefits, and protections unattainable through other means. While there are some benefits and protections that same-sex couples can achieve by hiring a lawyer to draw up scads of expensive legal documentation, there are no legal means for gay couples to approximate all of the rights achieved by a simple stroke of the pen upon the marriage license of a heterosexual couple. By paying a license fee somewhere between $20 and $80 (depending upon the state), heterosexual couples immediately gain 1000+ rights on both the state and federal level, while gay and lesbian couples must spend hundreds, even thousands of dollars in legal fees in order to gain even a small fraction of these benefits and protections.

These discussions can seems rather abstract for many heterosexual people who simply take for granted the rights and protections that were almost magically granted to them one cool summer evening when they giddily signed their marriage license, rushing on their way from the wedding ceremony to the reception. Allow me to provide a glimpse into the ways same-sex couples can suddenly and jarringly find themselves in precarious, vulnerable, and frightening situations without legal recognition and protection for their most intimate relationships.[3]

On numerous occasions, a gay or lesbian person has rushed to the emergency room of the local hospital after an accident has seriously threatened a partner's life, only to be sequestered in the lobby, unable to make important medical decisions or even to see their loved one, sometimes hanging on to the last moments of life. Even when gay couples produce medical power of attorney documents, these directives may simply be ignored at the discretion of medical staff who rely, instead, upon the wishes and desires of the patient's biological family to direct medical decisions.

In the already difficult time of a partner's death, often after decades of committed relationship, the grief-filled experience of many gay and lesbian people has been incomprehensibly exacerbated by biological family members — sometimes estranged for years — swooping in at the time of death to take possession of the body (and the estate).

Many grieving partners have even been kept away from funeral services for their loved ones who were mourned and buried in cities and towns they no longer regarded as "home."

When lesbian and gay couples have children, either from a previous heterosexual marriage or through adoption or artificial insemination, court rulings have regularly severed the relational rights of gay or lesbian parents and their children. In cases of heterosexual divorce, visitation rights have been denied a parent because she or he now lives in a lesbian or gay partnership. When one lesbian or gay partner has died, children have been taken from the other partner who holds no biological relation — despite having raised the child — and, instead, given over to the custody of more distant family members. In the past few decades, courts have frequently ruled against the parenting rights of gay and lesbian couples due to their sexual orientation. Historian George Chauncey notes, "Even when judges did not believe that a parent's homosexuality automatically disqualified her as a parent, they were likely to deny her custody because of the stigma they thought the children would endure if their peers learned the parent was gay."[4] Without the legal status of marriage, there is often very little successful recourse.

Many more heartrending narratives could be told about queer relationships encountering social and legal inequality with regard to immigration rights, healthcare and insurance coverage, taxation benefits, inheritance rights, wrongful death actions, confidential marital communications, shared property rights, and on and on.

Marriage equality is not about the ability to have third-party legitimation of queer relationships, or even attaining symbolic equality with straight couples in the public square. Marriage inequality is an "issue" that affects the everyday lives of lesbian and gay couples in ways that are utterly unimaginable for straight couples in our society. So I hope it is understandable — even for those who disagree — why many queer people find it necessary to continue the slow, grinding, relentless struggle for marriage equality. But the conversation cannot end there, else we miss out on opportunities to learn from the ways queer people have formed strong and lasting relationships amidst a legal and ecclesial climate that so steadily works against them.

An Autobiographical Interlude

While queer people in our society share many experiences in common, no two queer lives are alike and no two same-sex relationships are identical. My own narrative of queer life and relationship inevitably shapes my perspective on the question, "What can churches learn from queer people about the formation of relationships?" Some of these personal influences are well within my awareness, but some are sure to influence my perspectives from some place outside of conscious awareness. So for my own benefit and for that of the reader, it is important to spend a little time explaining myself.

Heterosexual children grow up in a world populated with heterosexual people — from parents, to church members, to television characters — heterosexual relationships between one man and one woman are the assumed "norm" in our society. Until fairly recently, it would be possible for a queer kid to go through the entirety of childhood and adolescence (as I did) without knowing even one person in a same-sex relationship. Queer children often grow up with very few, if any, examples of same-sex relationships to provide a picture of how one's own future relationships might take shape. This is changing, of course, but this is the reality in which a vast number of queer kids grow up.

In some sense, my own relationship with my partner, Ben, doesn't break many typical relational norms. Aside from the fact that we are both men, we have a story that is very similar to the relational narratives of many straight Christian couples. We met at a Baptist college where we both studied religion. We were in a weekly college Bible study together. We were involved in ministry together in local churches and our university's campus ministry. We were friends for two years before we started dating (it took us almost that long to "come out" to each other). And, to top it all off, our first actual date was to the religious art museum at Bob Jones University — one of the most conservative Christian universities in the country. Our relationship developed quite according to the plan laid out for us in the Southern Baptist churches of our upbringing — save for the conspicuous fact that we were both men.

One of the primary commonalities that drew us together in relationship was our commitment to Christ and the church, along with a shared sense of calling into ministry. What I identify as the emergence of my own calling to ministry started very early in my childhood and intersected in many ways with my emerging sense of sexuality. As a five-year-old, I was enamored with choral music, congregational hymn singing, and most especially the pipe organ. This led not only to my faithful childhood attendance in the Sunday service of my family's small town Baptist congregation, but also to a year of persistently begging my father and grandfather to build a church of my own in our backyard. Both contractors by trade, they finally relented and built a small chapel complete with a cross-adorned steeple and a stained-glass window. My grandmother sewed a robe and stole to fit my six-year-old stature. A woman in a neighboring town sold us her old electronic organ. My other grandfather was often enlisted to "preach" as I led the music for the mostly imaginary congregation.

It was during this same period of childhood that I remember first becoming aware of another newly emerging sense — an awareness of attraction to my male peers. While I also experienced an attraction to girls, I began noticing that I liked boys in the same way. Since I had never heard anyone talk about this phenomenon, I made sense of this attraction in several stages: First, I just assumed that everyone was attracted to both men and women but only formed romantic relationships with the "opposite" sex. Later, I began to figure out that this wasn't necessarily the case and perhaps I was, in some way, different from my peers. In my next phase of understanding, while I hadn't heard many people talk about same-sex attraction, I had heard enough to know that it wasn't looked upon kindly by church and society. So I prayed about this attraction in whatever childhood way I could manage until, after some years, the realization emerged that my sexuality wasn't a problem after all.

While I had come to the understanding that it wasn't a "problem" to be attracted to other men, I also knew I must keep it a secret. After all, growing up in my small South Carolina town, I did not know one single person who identified as gay, lesbian, bisexual, or transgender until well after I graduated high school and moved away to college. Isolation facilitates a great deal of secret keeping about sexuality.

But the other reason for my secret keeping (what many refer to as being "in the closet") was the tension that had become evident between my emerging sense of sexual identity and my emerging sense of call to ministry. By adolescence, I knew very well the pervasive attitudes of churches toward LGBTQ persons, and I knew my own pathway into ministry would be greatly hindered by my "coming out." So I kept my secret and proceeded on to service in the ministry of local churches. Eventually, after meeting Ben in college and long before we ever came out to each other and formed an intimate relationship, we served in ministry together both in our college campus ministry and in local congregations. And at least two years into our dating relationship, we were still keeping our sexuality and our relationship a secret from others while attending seminary and serving in ministry together on staff at a small Southern Baptist church. We knew that our love for one another might jeopardize our potential to fulfill our callings and, in reality, could put our very lives in jeopardy.

But while churches worked to keep us in the closet for a long time, a church also helped us to find freedom from secret keeping and isolation. It was another Baptist congregation, Oakhurst Baptist Church in Decatur, Georgia, where we first experienced not only a faith community, but also a community of any kind that celebrated our relationship and nurtured our ministerial callings, eventually ordaining us both into ministry.

My relationship with Ben doesn't break many typical norms and in many ways seems like a very safe narrative of same-sex love to recount in church. For this reason, Ben and I have often received congratulatory remarks, affirming the normalcy of our lives and relationship in ways that make it "easier for others to accept us." This feels something like I imagine it might feel for a non-native English speaker to be congratulated on being "so bright and articulate," as if speaking another language as one's native tongue automatically calls one's intelligence into question. Or perhaps something like it might feel for a racial minority to be congratulated as a "credit to your race" for some outstanding achievement — a complimentary veneer applied to the working assumption that simply being a member of one's racial group calls one's worth into question until one demonstrates an ability to live up to the imposed standards of the dominant racial norm. We have far more to learn from our differences than how to fit in or live up to the norms and standards of dominant groups — heterosexual, white, English-speaking, or otherwise.

Ethicist Kathy Rudy ruptures any sense of comfort we garner from rather normative relational narratives like my own when she argues, "Gay people today have become experts at impersonating straight nuclear families; the only thing that is different is that one of us is the wrong gender."[5] While my personal story informs my own approach to the theology and practice of intimate relationships, it is important to note that my own story should not be taken as a representative norm for the relationships of lesbian, gay, bisexual, and transgender persons, nor should it be considered as the only configuration of a covenanted relationship that holds instructive potential for churches on matters of relationship. In fact, the stories of more radical difference from the norm hold the potential to teach us the most.

Queer people should be wary of heterosexual impersonation, asking ourselves in whose image we are being formed and for what purpose. Just to get our slice of the pie (or at least the crumbs that fall from the table of heterosexual privilege)? Straight Christians should be equally alert in asking, "Are we only willing to learn from, appreciate, and affirm those who look, act, and live in ways that mirror our own ways of being?" Indeed, queer people have a great deal more to teach us about covenant than how to best "fit in" to a sexual and relational norm that is defined from a heterosexual perspective.

Preliminary Lessons from Same-Sex Relationships

As I quoted in the Introduction, Elizabeth Stuart reminds us, "The space of the marginalized is often a space where imagination can flourish outside the restricting dictates of the mainstream."[6] While the prejudice, marginalization, and violence that queer persons face in this country and around the world should not be viewed through rose-colored glasses, queer people have lived at the margins of the mainstream for a long time now and our imagination has flourished bountifully, informing our practice of relationship in ways not captured by simple debates over the definition of marriage. With the help of queer theologians and social theorists, let's now try to imagine some of the potential lessons we might learn if we were to appreciatively and compassionately explore the relationships of queer people; lessons not of how we should or ought to form relationships, but lessons pointing to the possibilities opened up to us for imagining intimate relationship beyond the dictates of the mainstream.

Questioning Gender Norms in Intimate Relationship

One of the most significant opportunities provided by queer lives is the ability of our example to help call into question a long history of patriarchal gender norms that linger to this day. What we often term "traditional" marital relationships in the U.S. — especially in Christian contexts — come with a host of culturally conditioned gender expectations that are imbued with unequal power relations between women and men. Theological ethicist, Margaret Farley, says about this history, "[T]raditional interpretations of heterosexual sex are steeped in images of the male as active and the female passive, the woman as receptacle and the man as fulfiller, the woman as ground and the man as seed."[7]

In her historical tracing of this patriarchal system, Gerda Lerner notes that the first known gender-defined role for women was the role of being exchanged in marriage transactions and, conversely, the first historical gender defined role for men was to set the terms of that exchange, much the same way men conducted transactions for the exchange of land. Similarly, in every historic society that practiced slavery, Lerner finds that female slaves were exploited as providers of sexual services and reproduction.[8] Of course, these practices of female sexual enslavement regularly continue to this day through widespread human trafficking.

This historical baggage of male dominance and female submission and servitude is not easily shed, even if we do see ourselves as more egalitarian in our modern versions of "traditional" marriage. Yet, when no predefined gender roles exist to unthinkingly guide how intimate relationships are to be fostered, the potential — at very least — is present for relationships forged not according to centuries of gender role residue (the majority of which has served to subjugate women to male dominance), but instead through commitments to mutuality and equality. While same-sex relationships are not immune to power inequalities, those in same-sex relationships must, of necessity, give explicit consideration to their preferred relational roles when the relationships are not formed between man and woman, but between two men or two women.

These considerations start with the ever-confusing questions straight people wonder to themselves about gay and lesbian relationships: Who does the dishes? How do you know who should pick up the check on a date? Who proposes to whom? But then moves on to grapple with more important questions, such as: Despite our cultural examples, how can a committed relationship be formed around an ideal of equality? In what ways does the ideal of mutuality influence the way we relate sexually? Which cultural lessons about what it means to be a "real man" or "real woman" do we wish to retain and which do we want to shed as undesirable cultural baggage that diminishes equality and mutuality in our relationship?

Choosing Ideals to Guide Our Relationships

Aside from challenging the many versions of patriarchy that infuse traditional concepts of heterosexual marriage, the lives and example of queer people can help us to question the ideals that guide the course of our intimate relationships. As mentioned above, relational commitments to mutuality and equality can more readily take shape when no predefined gender roles (e.g., "breadwinner," "caregiver," "leader," "homemaker," "spiritual head," etc.) are automatically overlaid onto our intimate bonds based solely upon gender divisions. The terminology that queer people often use to describe their most intimate relationships — "partners," for example — is suggestive of relational commitments to mutuality and equality. This term works to communicate these ideals in a way that "husband and wife" — or the more traditional "man and wife"[9] — often doesn't, due to centuries of cultural baggage defining the roles prescribed by these terms.

Similarly, pastoral theologian Joretta L. Marshall connects the relational ideal of mutuality to the equally important ideal of justice. Marshall defines justice in relationships as "the building of right relations between persons and communities where there is shared power, honest and open communication, and connection with others outside the primary relationship."[10] The questions queer examples provoke about relational mutuality, equality, and justice might lead churches to ask more critical questions than simply how to define or redefine the institution of marriage. Questions like: What examples are offered to us by our religious tradition that help us to form relational practices based on ideals of mutuality, equality, and justice? Whether between two women, two men, or a man and woman, what elements of our sacred texts and traditions continue to hinder us from forming relationships based upon these ideals?

Aside from the times when queer people are practicing their best heterosexual impersonations, queer lives and examples creatively disturb the commonsensical and all-too-easy ways our relationships fall neatly into a patterned script that we call traditional. The term, "traditional marriage," serves very little purpose beyond rhetorically removing any reason we might have to revisit and more carefully consider the ideals that best exemplify how to forge intimate relationships in Christian faithfulness.

Expanding our Relational Vocabulary

Social theorist Michael Warner points out, "There are almost as many kinds of relationship as there are people in combination . . . Most have no labels. Most receive no public recognition."[11] Warner continues,

> You will realize that only a fine and rapidly shifting line separates sexual culture from many other relations of durability and care. The impoverished vocabulary of straight culture tells us that people should be either husbands and wives or (nonsexual) friends. Marriage marks that line. It is not the way many queers live. If there is such a thing as a gay way of life, it consists in these relations, a welter of intimacies outside the framework of professions and institutions and ordinary social obligations. Straight culture has much to learn from it, and in many ways has already begun to learn from it. Queers should be insisting on teaching these lessons.[12]

Churches should be curious about what we might learn from this "welter of intimacies" and the proliferation of relational practices that simply cannot by captured by the easy categories of "married," "single," or the in-between of "not married but living together." Expanding our vocabularies for intimate relationships invites us to continually reimagine how these relationships are formed — embodying what norms, formed according to what standards, in light of what examples, and toward what relational ends? One possibility for expanding our relational vocabulary comes from queer theologians who name "friendship" as a guiding term for understanding intimate relationships.

In her book, *Just Good Friends*, Elizabeth Stuart argues that "a great many lesbian and gay people understand their committed sexual relationships not in the terms of marriage or of 'living together' like unmarried heterosexual couples, but in terms of friendship."[13] Stuart says that committed relationships conceived in these terms exemplify "that friendship is a relationship that can usually only exist between people who enjoy equal power relations."[14] Picking up on these same threads connecting covenantal partnerships and deep friendship, Marshall points out an experiential reality in many lesbian relationships, saying, "In the lesbian community, women often reflect this sentiment . . . by remaining friends even after the intensity of a physical or sexual relationship is over."[15]

These are not concerns of simple terminology substitution for the purpose of being more inclusive or less patriarchal in our speech. The language we use really matters, as it provides guiding images and metaphors that we draw upon to construct our understanding and practice of relationships. Churches that become intentionally curious about the possibilities for a new relational vocabulary opened to us by queer lives might find themselves asking: What terms do we habitually use to speak of intimate relationships that tend to go unexamined because we already believe we know the extent of their meaning (e.g., fidelity, intimacy, etc.)? How might an expanded vocabulary for intimate relationships help us to more intentionally and carefully name what we believe to be the important characteristics and ideals of committed relationship?

Rethinking Sex

Ethicist Kathy Rudy argues, "[T]he pertinent question is not which kind of partner or pattern is the only ethical one, but rather which kinds of sexual interventions change our lives and make us part of one another, which acts unite us into one body, which contexts fight meaninglessness."[16] Sex is often at the center of our debates over queer lives — particularly sex between gay men. From sodomy laws to what sex acts we presume the Bible condones and forbids, the particular sexual practices of queer people have often become the centerpiece of our conversation on sexual ethics. Though it is rarely acknowledged that nearly any of the practices in question are just as easily practiced by heterosexual couples as by queer persons.

Our discussions of sexuality must now begin to extend beyond permitting or forbidding the particulars of who does what to whom. Sex is far more multifaceted than our simple discussions would often lead us to believe — hence the reason our discussions of sex in church are not often helpful . . . to anyone. Margaret Farley makes the rich complexity of the subject clear, stating,

> [T]he motivations and aims of sex are as multiple as are its forms of embodiment and pleasure. For different individuals and on different occasions these can include a desire to enhance self-esteem, drive out depression and despair, express love and faithfulness, sustain a relationship or a marriage that is without mutual love, repay favors, escape into recreation and play, reveal one's intimate self and attain access to the intimate self of another, earn a living, and on and on.[17]

But if the motivations and aims of sex are really this vast, why have our churches' discussions about sexuality centered almost exclusively upon only two concerns: whether or not your sexual partner is of a different sex and whether or not the two of you are married? If churches seized the critical moment provided by queer lives and examples to rethink sex altogether, we might begin asking: How do our churches' teachings on sex unnecessarily limit the discussion, leaving our most important questions and concerns unaddressed? Whose lives are regularly omitted from our discussions of sexuality (e.g., single people, elderly people, etc.)? Even within what we deem the "appropriate" forms of relationship, how can sex still fail to live up to ideals of mutuality and equality and instead be practiced in ways that harm relationship?[18]

Organizing Life Beyond Gender Divisions

There have always been religious groups zeroing in on a few particular passages of the Bible, clinging to them with dogged persistence, and practicing them with as much simple literalism as they can manage. Men's long beards, women's head coverings, abstaining from certain foods, prohibitions on alcohol or dancing, exclusively a cappella singing in worship — all these examples and more represent people of faith trying to take particular passages of scripture as seriously and literally as they know how. While I'm not endorsing the biblical interpretive strategies that lead to these practices, the persistence of these groups in practicing the meaning they believe these scriptures hold does spark my curiosity.

These examples cause me to imagine the community that might take shape if a church or religious group became obsessive about putting in to practice, as literally as possible, the passage from Galatians 3: "As many of you as were baptized into Christ have clothed yourselves with Christ. There is no longer Jew or Greek, there is no longer slave or free, *there is no longer male and female*, for all of you are one in Christ Jesus" (vv. 27-28, emphasis mine). No longer male and female . . . What would this community of faith look like? How would their lives be organized if guided by a rigidly literal interpretation of this passage?

By this, I don't mean to imagine a situation when we no longer acknowledge gender as an important part of our experience as humans. I simply mean to invite imagination into the possibilities of an unwavering commitment to divesting ourselves of divvying up roles and responsibilities, rights and privileges, relationships and social customs based upon gendered divisions.[19] In questioning the relevance of these gender divisions for our lives and our churches, we stand to learn the most from the lives and examples of bisexual and transgender people.

Bisexual people — whose emotional, physical, and sexual attraction is felt for both women and men — are living signs of the rich complexity of sexuality that isn't often reflected in our discussion of the subject.[20] There are a lot of bisexual men who are happily married to women, but who dare not openly acknowledge their experience of attraction to both women and men, else they invite the same stigma that many churches heap upon the heads of gay and lesbian people. The same goes for bisexual women happily married to men. Likewise, there are many same-sex partnered people who do not speak of their bisexual attractions in queer company, lest they be accused of "fence sitting" or being "unable to make up their minds." These experiences point to the discomfort we have with bisexual realities and our attempt to assuage this discomfort by forcing binary, either/or categorizations upon people: Either you are straight or you are gay. But what might the example of bisexual people — who form relationships based not upon the gender of their partner, but upon a myriad of other qualities sparking their attraction — teach us all about limits of our simplistic, binary, straight/gay understandings of human sexuality? If the gender of a person isn't a determinative factor in the potential for forming a committed relationship, what other considerations might we begin to talk about as important to the formation of intimate bonds?

Likewise, transgender people — whose psychological and spiritual sense of gender differs from the social and cultural expectations attached to the biological/physical sex characteristics with which they were born — are living signs of the rich diversity of gender experience and embodiment that we often fail to appreciate. Whether transgender persons choose (and are able to afford) to complete a gender reassignment process (a surgical and hormonal transition from male to female or from female to male) or simply choose to live against the grain of the gendered expectations foisted upon them at birth, their lives can be instructive examples to churches, prompting the questions: How many of our church programs and activities do we base upon a presumed, unambiguous, experience of either male or female gender? How do we train our children from the nursery on with subtle lessons on what it means to be either a boy or a girl (e.g., the colors they should like, the toys they should play with, the roles they should have in a play or pageant, etc.)?[21]

Bisexual and transgender lives, more than any other, can help us all to imagine the possibilities of organizing our churches, communities, and society beyond the roles and responsibilities, rights and privileges, relationships and social customs we so often base solely upon gendered divisions. Perhaps there is even something intensely biblical about the way bisexual and transgender people live against the simplistic divisions of sexual orientation as either straight or gay and gender as either male or female unambiguously assigned at birth.

I call these preliminary lessons because the lessons we all stand to learn from paying careful, appreciative attention to queer lives are far too numerous and diverse to be contained within the space of a few pages. In order to learn the lessons queer lives have to offer us about the formation and practice of relationship, churches must learn to cultivate a more robust compassionate curiosity into the beauty and complexity of human life.

Cultivating New Conversations in Churches

Imagine that your church assembled a panel of experts to lead a forum on sexual orientation for your congregation. Let's say each presenter was asked to talk from their particular area of expertise about each side of the same-sex marriage debate. The overarching question might be something like, "Should same-sex couples be allowed to marry?" You might invite a biblical scholar, a legal expert, a theologian, a psychologist, and perhaps a few others to weigh in on the subject, trying to get a balanced perspective from all sides. They might address the litany of our usual concerns: "Why are people gay — nature or nurture?" "Can sexual orientation be changed?" "What does the Bible say about homosexuality?" "How do we understand traditional, biblical marriage?"

Now imagine an entirely different forum. This time, imagine
what a church might learn about the practices of relationship if it set
aside a time to intentionally bracket questions of the religious and/or
legal legitimacy of same-sex relationships and spent some time with a
multi-generational group of willing and thoughtful queer folks, reflec-
tively and appreciatively asking questions like these:

- How did you come to understand your relationship with your partner as committed or covenanted when your own churches or families
  or communities refused to recognize your partnership in this way?

- How did you cultivate communities that recognized the importance
  of your covenant with one another when most churches and states
  do not recognize the legitimacy of your bond? How did these communities support the growth of your relationship? In light of this,
  how can churches become better supportive communities for your
  relationship?

- If the typical marriage ceremony wasn't an option or wasn't of interest
  to you, what rituals, signs, and symbols of your relationship became
  important to you and why?

- As you grew up observing the example of straight couples, what qualities and attributes of these relationships did you wish to emulate
  and what qualities and attributes did you decide you'd rather leave
  behind?

- Without a marriage recognized by the state, how did you work
  out all of the things (rights and protections, etc.) that heterosexual
  people take for granted? What rights, protections, and benefits have
  you still been unable to access in your relationship due to the lack of
  legal recognition?

- When you broke up with former partners, did you manage to ami-
  cably separate without the aid of lawyers and divorce proceedings? If

so, how? Did anything about that process better allow you to remain friends with your former partner after you separated?

• What biblical models have you drawn upon to understand how to form your relationship in ways that are faithful to your Christian commitment?

What vastly different discussions would flow from these two kinds of forums! If the congregation involved in these discussions was comprised of members who already disagreed about the legitimacy of same-sex marriages, you can be sure that many would leave either of these two forums still holding to their divergent views. But beyond the different "positions" represented among attendees, imagine the possibilities for rich discussion and understanding that might flow from the second type of discussion where queer people are treated as teachers who have something to share with a compassionately curious audience. The first scenario, instead, treats queer people as subjects being scrutinized by amassing the right information and forming opinions about their lives, even without any first-hand experience of the lives in question. Beyond leaving with the ideas and arguments proffered by the so-called expert panel — some supporting and others criticizing same-sex marriage — the panel of queer respondents offers a first-person account of lessons learned at the margins, where imagination flourishes outside dictates of the taken-for-granted mainstream and all are offered the opportunity to enrich their own lives and relational possibilities.[22]

To be sure, reframing the discussion in this way doesn't offer a way out of having to make up one's mind about the legitimacy question surrounding same-sex marriage. When we go into the voting booth or enter into deliberation within our congregations and denominations over this question, we will have to decide how to address the questions in faithfulness to our understanding of either the constitution (in the case of legal questions) or Christian faith (in the case of religious questions). What the second scenario offers, then, is not a middle way of intentional indecision over the questions of same-sex marriage. Instead, it opens up to us a cadre of questions we will simply never ask if our sole concern is the legality or Christian legitimacy of same-sex marriage. It is from these more expansive, imaginative and compassionately curious questions that we stand to learn the most as churches striving to faithfully cultivate practices of relationship and covenant.

What Should *Really* Trouble Churches
about Marriage Debates

Witnessing the frothing tizzy so many preachers get worked into over the topic of gay marriage, I have come to wonder if perhaps we are missing the most troubling aspect of the whole discussion. Rather than the imagined threat to marriage lodged by gay couples seeking to wed, churches might instead be troubled by the relational idols we so fiercely cling to in these debates.

In much Christian discourse on the subject of marriage and covenant, we have idolized particular configurations of relationship — primarily that configuration of the heterosexual nuclear family. Our battles over family values have become little more than attempts to maintain the idolized status of this man-woman-children configuration of relationship and the power that comes with exclusive legal legitimacy. Single-parent families, cultural practices of close-knit extended families often living under the same roof, and same-sex families are relegated to second-class status allowed only to strive in living up to the heterosexual ideal/idol of the nuclear family.

In the same way, same-sex relationships should not be idolized. They have the potential for many of the same ills suffered by straight couples, such as domestic violence, and emotional abuse. Same-sex relationships do, however, invite us to move beyond relationship idols to relational ideals. They invite us into more intentional reflection upon the theological, ethical and biblical ideals toward which our covenantal relationships (same-sex or different-sex) might strive. But the queer questioning about the definition of marriage should also lead us to move beyond our boundary maintenance, to ask even more fundamental questions about how the institution of marriage is practiced in our society.

Churches and queer people must continue to question whether marriage equality for same-sex couples is really the final solution to the inequities embedded in our current social and legal conceptions of marriage. For example, we might continue to question why so many of the rights, financial benefits, and relational protections to which we have access in the U.S. are available only through the institution of marriage.

We might find ourselves troubled by the ways financial and social benefits that attend the institution of marriage work to the detriment of the never married, the not-yet-married, and those who do not wish to be married. We should continue to ask what other configurations of relationship — for example, unmarried siblings, a widowed parent and unmarried child, life-long non-sexual companions, etc. — exhibit all of the characteristics of commitment to mutual well-being and protection, life-long caretaking and companionship, partnership, etc., yet are made vulnerable without a social/legal relationship status that affords them the rights, benefits, and protections that married couples enjoy without question.

For churches, this means taking the conversation beyond debating the definition of marriage, to a prophetic critique of the ways our government and society privilege one configuration of relationship with a host of benefits and incentives — financial benefits pertaining to health care and taxation, for example — while leaving anyone outside of this configuration lacking. Aside from the rights, financial benefits, and mutual protections afforded to citizens almost exclusively through the institution of marriage, Michael Warner reminds us of the social privileging of the institution, saying, "Whether they like it or not, married people have countless privileges, some that define marriage and some that ought to have nothing to do with it. They are taken more seriously than unmarried people; they are more likely to be invited to dinner parties, offered jobs, and elected to public office. In short, they have status."[23]

When we think about these concerns in light of our faith, we should be troubled by all of the ways churches continue to privilege marriage to the detriment of other forms of relationship. Our theological imaginations and our religious airtime have been overly occupied with a singular focus upon marriage. This despite the Bible's persistent concern for those outside of this institution — for example, instructions for the communal care of widows and orphans (James 1:17). Our curiosity might be sparked by the example of Jesus himself, remaining unmarried and taking up life with a community of twelve men whose dying moments even included this relational-stretching vignette from John: "When Jesus saw his mother and the disciple whom he loved standing beside her, he said to his mother, 'Woman, here is your son.' Then he said to the disciple, 'Here is your mother.' And from that hour the disciple took her into his own home" (John 19:26-27). We might look again at the passage from Mark quoted in the Introduction: When his mother and brothers sent a messenger into the crowd to retrieve him, Jesus asked the messenger, "Who are my mother and my brothers?" (Mark 3:33).

The point of mentioning these biblical passages and vignettes isn't to prove anything about "what the Bible says" about the right way to practice relationship. But one lesson we might take from these provocative biblical passages is this: There is more to relatedness than we have recognized in our typical debates over marriage. Churches and queer people alike have frequently reduced a rich tapestry of human relatedness to one single question: "Should same-sex couples be allowed to marry?" In single-mindedly clinging to this question, not only do we risk losing sight of the potential to learn from same-sex relationships that have been historically forged outside the sanction of legal and ecclesial marital bonds, but we also risk the further marginalization of those who do not, will not, and cannot form these bonds — whether queer or straight. Urvashi Vaid compellingly argues,

> [G]ay civil rights must be seen as part of a broader focus
> on human rights, sexual and gender equality, social

and economic justice, and faith in a multiracial society . . . Our movement must strive beyond personal
gain to an institutional transformation, beyond mainstreaming ourselves into the center to transforming the
mainstream.[24]

Queer lives continually call into question the privileged status of
heterosexual marriage. But beyond questioning the boundaries of marriage, we must become more attentive to the ways our communities of
faith mirror, reproduce and invent still more ways of elevating the social
status of the married couple — straight or gay — while passively ignoring or actively demeaning other forms of relationship that may have as
much, if not more, to teach us about relational practices than we could
ever learn from the privileged heterosexual nuclear family alone.

Notes

[1]Legal marriage for same-sex couples is no insignificant or merely symbolic matter as the Human Rights Campaign notes that there are 1,138 benefits,
rights and protections provided on the basis of marital status in Federal law. See "An
Overview of Federal Rights and Protections Granted to Married Couples," Human
Rights Campaign, accessed February 7, 2013, http://www.hrc.org/resources/entry/
an-overview-of-federal-rights-and-protections-granted-to-married-couples.

[2]Notably, there are a number of queer theorists who have been very active in
writing about these relational alternatives, but the "mainstream" message of the gay rights
movement in the past two decades, powered by its largest and wealthiest organizations,
has been aimed toward the legalization of same-sex marriage.

[3]For readers interested in greater detail and historical case examples, George
Chauncey thoroughly but accessibly documents the historical evolution of the struggle
for marriage equality in the U.S. He provides a brief, readable history explaining what is
at stake in debates over marriage equality for gay and lesbian couples, providing a brief

history of antigay discrimination and gay rights in the U.S. over the last century. George Chauncey, *Why Marriage? The History Shaping Today's Debate Over Gay Equality* (New York: Basic Books, 2004).

[4]Chauncey, *Why Marriage?*, 107.

[5]Kathy Rudy, *Sex and the Church: Gender, Homosexuality, and the Transformation of Christian Ethics* (Boston: Beacon, 1997), 75.

[6]Elizabeth Stuart, *Just Good Friends: Towards a Lesbian and Gay Theology of Relationships* (New York: Mowbray, 1995), 5.

[7]Margaret A. Farley, *Just Love: A Framework for Christian Sexual Ethics* (New York: Continuum, 2010), 221. Farley's text is perhaps the most accessible and thorough treatment of Christian sexual ethics to enter the ongoing conversation and provides a helpful resource to congregations and individuals interested in deepening the sophistication of dialogue on sexual ethics.

[8]Gerda Lerner, *The Creation of Patriarchy* (New York: Oxford University Press, 1986), 214.

[9]Chauncey notes that, historically, the "marriage ceremony pronounced the couple 'man and wife' because the man's legal status changed so little compared to the woman's." *Why Marriage?*, 67.

[10]Joretta L. Marshall, *Counseling Lesbian Partners* (Louisville: Westminster John Knox, 1997), 57.

[11]Michael Warner, *The Trouble with Normal: Sex, Politics, and the Ethics of Queer Life* (New York: The Free Press, 1999), 115-16.

[12]Warner, *The Trouble with Normal*, 116.

[13]Stuart, *Just Good Friends*, 28.

[14]Stuart, *Just Good Friends*, 43.

[15]Marshall, *Counseling Lesbian Partners*, 52.

[16]Kathy Rudy, *Sex and the Church: Gender, Homosexuality, and the Transformation of Christian Ethics* (Boston: Beacon Press, 1997), 83.

[17]Farley, *Just Love*, 163.

[18]Some of these questions were addressed in a conference titled, "A [Baptist] Conference on Sexuality and Covenant," hosted by the Cooperative Baptist Fellowship and Mercer University in April 2012. The printed proceedings of this conference, including each plenary address, can be accessed in a special issue of *Christian Ethics Today*

20(4) (Fall 2012), accessible online at http://christianethicstoday.com/wp/wp-content/ uploads/2011/02/40680_Journal-88-Special1.pdf.

[19]Some of this imaginative theological work is performed by Virginia Ramey Mollenkott in her text, *Omnigender: A Trans-religious Approach*, revised and expanded (Cleveland: Pilgrim, 2007).

[20]Time and time again I hear pastors wrongly describe "bisexuality" as the desire to have more than one sexual relationship at a time. While bisexual people, just like straight or gay people, may very well have more than one sexual relationship at a time, this is *not* what the term "bisexuality" means. The term simply describes people who experience physical, emotional, and spiritual *attraction* to both men and women. The term suggests nothing about *what kind* of relationships this person forms, whether a life-long monogamous relationship with a person of the same sex, a life-long monogamous relationship with a partner of a different sex, serial monogamy, polygamy, life-long celibacy, etc.

[21]Churches — even those open and affirming of gay and lesbian people — often have a limited understanding of transgender lives and concerns. In addition to *Omnigender* cited in the note above, churches may find a helpful resource in Justin Tanis, *Trans-Gendered: Theology, Ministry, and Communities of Faith* (Cleveland: Pilgrim, 2003).

[22]If a congregation decided to organize such a forum, I recommend giving the queer participants that are invited ample time in advance of the forum to reflect upon the questions being posed. Not only are many of the principles we select to guide our relationships not entirely conscious but are, instead, lived into over time, but there is also a shift in queer mindset necessitated by this type of appreciative, compassionate inquiry. Normally, the questions religious communities pose to us about our relationships are far more suspiciously scrutinizing, rather than compassionately inquisitive. Thus, queer people must also prepare to shift our positions in such a conversation from *objects of study* to *active teachers* who have lived into vast sources of wisdom on the practice of relationship and covenant.

[23]Warner, *The Trouble with Normal*, 109. Readers interested in further reading on this argument should also see Janet R. Jakobsen, "Queer Relations: A Reading of Martha Nussbaum on Same-Sex Marriage," *Columbia Journal of Gender and Law* 19(1) (2010): 133-177.

[24]Urvashi Vaid, *Virtual Equality: The Mainstreaming of Gay & Lesbian Liberation* (New York: Anchor Books, 1995), 180.

Chapter Two

Lessons on Community

The faithful community gathers as a small group on the margins of society, regularly drawing the ire of authorities seeking to quash their way of life — often through violence. In the throes of persecution, they band together as a community, developing secret code words and symbols in order to identify themselves to one another while remaining anonymous to those who wish to do them harm. They follow a moral code that draws suspicion from their neighbors and suppression from the authorities. They exist as a subculture; meeting in secret at locations designated in advance as safe and free from the gaze of authorities. In spite of all safety measures and the close-knit care of those in the community, some are still caught and imprisoned while others are lost to violence — martyred for living against the grain of religious and governmental authority.

To the minds of many readers, this vignette aptly describes the earliest Christian community — persecuted by the Roman Empire and socially marginalized for the practice of their faith, banding together in tight-knit community. But this vignette just as accurately describes communities of queer people in the early-to-mid-twentieth century in the United States — especially in a handful of major U.S. cities.[1] One group of people this description does not characterize is U.S. Christians in the twenty-first century. So if we still have lessons to learn about the formation of community within the marginalizing and persecutory circumstances faced by the early Christian community, then the lives of queer people have much to teach us, as their experiences of community in the past century have mirrored these circumstances with far more striking similarity than have the experiences of most Christian congregation in the United States.

Without glorifying the situation of either the earliest Christians or queer people in prior eras of U.S history, the situational similarities faced by these two groups should raise the curiosity of churches enough to ask,

What can congregations learn from the example of queer people who have cultivated community at the margins of church and society?

In order to learn from queer examples of community, we must employ an attitude of compassionate curiosity, becoming familiar with recent queer experience in the United States. We inquire into these experiences of queer community so that, through them, churches may begin to see queer expressions of community as living examples from which to learn rather than a threat from which to run.

Cultivating Community at the Margins: A Brief Historical Sketch

Beyond the Stonewall riots and the assassination of Harvey Milk, most congregations — and many queer people, for that matter — know very little about queer history in the United States.[2] The history of LGBTQ movements isn't taught in most school curricula and there is little way to ensure the transmission of these stories through the generations of queer people. Many readers were probably even taken aback by the suggestion that the opening vignette is descriptive of queer experience in the mid-twentieth century. But experiences of marginalization and violence are far from fictional and serve as the very real social context for many of the communities that have been formed by queer people at the margins of church and society.

While same-sex sexuality and the transcending of a male/female biological gender binary have been features of many societies and cultures for millennia, the identification of a particular subgroup in society based upon sexual acts or embodied gender variance is a relatively recent phenomenon. At the point in history when queer people found themselves not only identified as a subgroup by their sexual preferences and gender identifications but also marginalized because of them, the formation of community began to become a necessity like never before. But before communities could form, queer people first had to find one another.

Finding One Another

Beginning the story in the late 1800s United States,[3] it was the thrust of industrial capitalism and the attending population shifts from a largely rural society into concentrated urban centers of industry that brought many gay and lesbian people into closer contact. While the cooperative labor of family life on the farm prevented many from ever pursuing their same-gender love, population shifts into economic centers of industry created a context in which those who experienced same-sex attraction could begin to imagine pursuing same-sex relationships.[4]

But it was the change wrought by a country at war that solidified the social context necessary for increased community among queer folk. During the Second World War, the segregation of sexes — with men at war and women employed in a variety of jobs outside of the home — placed many gay and lesbian people in contact with others who shared their sexual interest in members of the same sex, often for the first time. The geographic mobility of military life allowed soldiers to visit cities to which they would one day return in post-war years in order to pursue same-sex relationships that would have been virtually impossible in rural locales. Likewise, increasing opportunities for work outside the home opened possibilities for women to imagine a life of economic independence from men.

As evidence of the impact of these shifts, in the years immediately following World War II, the number of gay and lesbian bars dramatically increased in cities across the country and novels with gay and lesbian themes began to appear in greater number.[5] But the social shifts that brought about a more amenable climate for the formation of queer communities wasn't without its dangers for gays and lesbians forming bonds of same-sex intimacy. Both the stigma attached to same-sex love and the consequences for openly pursuing it were grave.

The Sick Sinful Criminal

While same-sex sexual acts have a long history of being viewed as evidence of sinful proclivities or infirmity of mind, in the decades following World War II, the discourses of religion, law, and psychiatry began to converge upon gay and lesbian lives in an insidious fashion. In the fifteen years following the War, more than half of state legislatures relied upon prevalent psychiatric explanations for homosexuality in order to pass "sexual psychopath laws that officially recognized homosexuality as a socially threatening disease."[6] But even the reclassification of homosexuality as a disease — rather than a simple act of immorality — didn't ease the suffering regularly imparted by lengthy prison sentences. Now, with the weight of psychiatric understandings, families began committing their gay members to asylums where treatments ranged from hypnosis and psychotherapy to castration, hysterectomy, lobotomy, electroshock, aversion therapy, and experimental drug treatments.[7] No longer a sinful act, homosexuality was transformed into a pathological identity necessitating psychiatric treatment to fix and requiring the force of law to curtail its damaging effects upon society.

As Kenneth Wald notes, "When the expression of physical intimacy between consenting adults of the same sex carries the threat of incarceration, it suggests the depth of social hostility to gays and lesbians and the willingness to embody it in law."[8] The legal embodiment of prevailing social hostility toward gays and lesbians was quite comprehensive. Even activities as innocent as dancing with someone of the same gender or wearing clothes supposed to have been worn by the other gender were looked upon by the police and the courts as forms of degenerate and disorderly conduct posing so dangerous a threat to social order that they merited imprisonment and fines.[9] At times, even the mere presence of gays and lesbians rendered an establishment disorderly and out of compliance with the law, placing a bar's license to serve alcohol in jeopardy if it so much as served a homosexual.[10]

In the 1950s, sexual perversion (i.e., homosexuality) became grounds for disbarment and dismissal from federal jobs, barring 1,700 people from federal employment from 1947 through the mid-50s.[11] The FBI compiled data on homosexuals including places they frequented. Even friendship with known gays and lesbians could subject one to investigation — placing one's livelihood and public reputation in jeopardy. In D.C., arrests of gays and lesbians in the early 1950s surpassed 1,000 per year, misdemeanor charges in Philadelphia averaged 100 per month, and Iowa's sexual psychopath law allowed for the committal of twenty-nine men to asylums without trial or conviction.[12] While the social context of large cities allowed for greater contact among queer people, the penalties surrounding these newfound relational possibilities were quite severe and called for more intentional forms of community and mutual support.

Forming Communities

It is possible that without the persistent legal, psychiatric, and religious forces brought to bear upon queer lives, a community may never have formed around commonalities of sexual orientation or gender identity. But these constraining forces gradually elicited the response of gays and lesbians who began organizing to slowly and steadily change the social discourse about the meaning of same-sex attraction. The two earliest organizations to emerge were the Mattachine Society, founded in Los Angeles in 1951 and comprised primarily of gay men, and the Daughters of Bilitis, emerging in 1955 as an organization for lesbian members. Both of these groups began in a rather secretive fashion, working to preserve the anonymity of the membership at a time when exposure meant the threat of converging forces of law, religion, and psychiatry.

Before they could begin reshaping larger societal views of gays and lesbians, however, they first needed to offer support and education to one another. Individuals who joined these groups helped one another shed a self-understanding as criminal or pathological and cultivated increasing awareness about the damaging effects of the culture's exclusionary and oppressive practices. While some within the emerging movements took the stance of defiant pride in their sexual identity, the central thrust of both groups was toward gaining respect in the eyes of heterosexual society and accommodation into social institutions.[13] These groups gradually began to take on a more public role, finding allies among professionals — sociologists, psychotherapists, and ministers — and reeducating the public in a way that began to very slowly diminish a view of gays and lesbians as sick, sinful, social deviants. But as these communities of gays and lesbians worked little by little toward these laudable ends, they achieved only a modicum of success in changing laws that criminalized queer relationships and social gatherings. Thus, other communities began to form around more radical, activist methods.

Working Toward Rights

The civil rights movement of the 1950s and 60s paved the way for a social climate in which a gay rights movement could emerge. Gays and lesbians learned through the example of civil rights leaders how to become activists. Not only did the civil rights movement pave the way for more direct forms of activism, but it also produced black lesbian and gay figures that played leading roles in both movements[14] — leaders like Bayard Rustin, a black gay man and civil rights activist who became a close advisor to Martin Luther King, Jr. and is credited with facilitating King's commitments to the nonviolent philosophy of Gandhi.[15]

Two decades of work by groups like Mattachine and the Daughters of Bilitis served to gradually alter the mentality of society toward its gay and lesbian members, struggling diligently with professionals and lawmakers to change discriminatory practices that targeted queer people. But far more was needed in order for lasting change to occur. The civil rights movement provided an example of activist strategies and leaders who knew how to employ them. In this historical light, the events of the Stonewall riots start to look less like the beginning of the gay rights narrative and more like a new chapter in the movement's story.

Stonewall and Activism

Long before it was trendy for churches to meet in bars, queer people were forming community there. So in the early morning of June 28, 1969, when the police raided the gay bar known as the Stonewall Inn in Greenwich Village — yet another target in a lengthy attempt to quell "disorderly" gatherings of gays and lesbians — the community resisted. As the patrons were disbanded, the group of largely young, nonwhite gays and lesbians along with a number of drag queens began the riots that would "spark a nationwide grassroots 'liberation' effort among gay men and women."[16] It is in the wake of this grassroots activism that the gay rights movement became an example of community as catalyst for large-scale social change.

AIDS and Communities of Care and Advocacy

But after the fervor surrounding Stonewall began to wane, it was the advent of the AIDS crisis in the 1980s that led queer people to begin forming communities that were exemplars of mutual care in the face of a largely uncaring society. For those of us not personally faced with the reality of AIDS at the height of the crisis of the 1980s, it may be difficult to imagine the terror and uncertainty induced by the myriad of early unknowns surrounding the disease. While the momentum of Stonewall had gradually diminished, the high mortality rates of gay people from a largely mysterious disease demonstrated that the need for community was never greater.

Urvashi Vaid describes the impact of AIDS on broadening the work of gay and lesbian rights organizations, which "suddenly became

engaged in building local gay and lesbian institutions — service organizations that became centers for gay men and lesbians to meet, work,
and take care of one another."[17] Chauncey describes the ground-level
communities of care that formed, saying, "In the city's dance clubs, bath-
houses, and cruising areas, many men had developed strong friendships
with other gay men who rallied around them when they became ill."[18]
At a time when government attention toward AIDS was either punitive
or altogether lacking and the mainstream press refused to provide seri-
ous coverage of the AIDS crisis,[19] queer people formed the communities
of mutual support that cared for the sick and dying, planned countless
funerals and memorials for loved ones whose biological families had
abandoned them, and founded the organizations that would mount the
most effective and meaningful response to the disease.

In light of this brief historical sketch, it is easy to see why historian John D'Emilio says, "[I]n a generation in which jeremiads about the
collapse of community in America are commonplace, many gay men and
lesbians have become the repository of vital wisdom about valuing and
maintaining a vigorous communal life."[20] The remainder of this chapter
will take a closer look at the example of queer communities as sources of
mutual care and as catalysts for social change, ending with a reflection
upon some of the more difficult questions surrounding the place of unity
within community.

Out of Isolation: Communities of Mutual Care

In an era when avenues for interpersonal communication pro-
liferate, many still experience a deep sense of isolation from others and a
void of close community ties. The overwhelming isolation that engulfs
so many lives is an experience familiar to many queer people, and we've

collectively learned a great deal through our emergence from isolation through the cultivation of community. These are lessons churches would do well to learn. As Kathy Rudy observes, "In America today, because being Christian is generally socially acceptable and without risk, we do not depend on the support of other parishioners in a way that makes us part of them."[21] Queer experiences of community hold the potential to help churches cut through the cultural elevation of individualist ideals that guide contemporary society. They also challenge the over-privileging of the nuclear family as the expression of communal relationship to the diminishment of other important forms of life-in-community.

Isolation is not unfamiliar to queer people. Most every queer person experiences isolation at some point in life, usually beginning at an early age. D'Emilio describes isolation as a "defining feature of gay experience," pointing to "the fact that almost all gay men and lesbians are neither raised in nor socialized at an early age into a gay community."[22] He goes on to say,

> The imprint of those critical years of isolation, especially when compounded by the historic invisibility of homo-sexuality in everyday social life and in popular culture, creates an insistent need for the alternative — for vis-ibility and the connection that community provides.[23]

Unlike children of many other minority groups, queer people are not born into a family and a community network of others who share their embodiment of difference and can prepare them for experiences of injustice and violence. A young girl most likely grows up with a mother, aunts, grandmothers and close female friends who populate her life with examples of adult women, who know the experience of life in a male-dominated society, and who can teach her important lessons about the difference between loving touch and sexual violence. An African American child most likely grows up with a family and community of others — adults and children — who share the child's racial identity, who will pass on and celebrate important pieces of African American heritage, and teach the child difficult lessons about navigating life in a racist society. But biological families and community networks rarely operate this way for queer people.

For numerous queer people, the family of origin turns very suddenly from a source of support into a source of scorn. Perhaps the most poignant example in my own experience of ministry was a teenage boy who confided in his mother about his attraction to other men and was immediately kicked out of his home during his final semester of high school. Despite attempts to remain in school until graduation, the instability of his newfound homelessness meant having to drop out only a couple of months from graduation in order to support himself.

This story — while heartbreaking and infuriating — is all too common. The National Gay and Lesbian Task Force issued a 2006 report suggesting that between 20 and 40 percent of all homeless youth identify as lesbian, gay, bisexual, or transgender. This is far greater than the percentage of LGBT-identified people in the U.S. population as a whole — a number probably closer to five percent. Not surprisingly, family conflict was the primary cause for a queer kid's loss of a stable home.[24]

Many queer young people in similar situations find shelter, emotional and economic support, and much needed community in people beyond their biological family. These bonds between queer persons are formed not out of sexual desire for one another or even out of the shared experience of a queer identity. Instead, these relational bonds are formed out of circumstances of marginalization that are transformed into experiences of mutual care and support — into a picture of genuine community. Even when the circumstances of one's family of origin are extraordinarily positive, there is often still a lack of close connection to other queer people who share similar social and developmental experiences related to one's sexual or gender identity — others who know firsthand the experience of social stigma and marginalization, as well as the joys of queer life and love. These isolating experiences often give rise to unique experiences of community as sources of mutual care and support among queer people.

Exemplars of community as sources of mutual care emerged throughout the last century as queer people formed organizations like the Mattachine Society and the Daughters of Bilitis to help individuals extricate themselves from the psychological tyranny of psychiatric views of the homosexual as mentally ill or socially deviant. Community as source of mutual care emerged with even greater ferocity when friends and loved ones began dying in droves from AIDS. These communities not only cared for their sick and dying, but also organized the efforts that would turn more and more societal attention and governmental resources toward fighting the disease. Far from the sinister gay agenda so often imagined to shape the machinations of queer organizing, the majority of these communities started in circumstances of very real human need. They formed around individuals seeking mutual care and support in the presence of a society intent on enforcing a program of shame and silence upon queer lives.

Through these examples, queer persons help us to recover a way of being in community that is true to a very historic commitment of the Christian tradition. As Kathy Rudy reminds us,

> The church has historically attempted to break down the boundaries that exist around primary, particular relationships in favor of relationships and dependencies on a community of believers. Christians throughout the centuries have understood that life in Christ means being responsible to and for many more people than one's spouse and children. Life in Christ, in the most radical sense, demands an openness to other community members.[25]

Many examples of queer commitment to relationship-in-community bare a similarity to the earliest iterations of the Christian church, holding all things in common and experiencing mutuality of care amid rejection of family, friends, and society. Aside from the examples in queer history, these expressions of community as source of mutual care take shape when queer people form chosen families outside the confines of biology, when genetics aren't enough to ensure lasting connection and sustaining care. Communities of care can be witnessed every day in the many LGBTQ teen shelters in major U.S. cities that house, feed, and educate the extraordinary number of queer teenagers being abused, rejected, or forced out of their homes at unconscionable rates.[26]

But in an era of comfortable U.S. Christianity, is the need for community as a life-preserving source of sustenance and care merely a footnote in the "triumphant" history of the Christian church? In a time now beginning to pass — when attendance in a Sunday service was a given for the majority of the U.S. population, when church membership elevated one's status in the community and one's hopes of getting elected to public office without it were nil — many churches had their collective memories of community at the margins slowly erased. Time moves on and contexts change, but the need for congregations to attend to the historic role of Christian community as a source of mutual care must not be eclipsed by individualistic cultural ideologies or contemporary Christianity's myopic focus upon defending the heterosexual nuclear family as *the* model of relatedness-in-community.

It isn't that queer people are better at practicing community the way Christians are supposed to do it. Instead, queer communities hold a mirror up to churches, reminding them of their heritage of communal care and beckoning them toward greater reflection of this heritage in contemporary iterations of Christian community. Inspired by this reflection, churches may begin to ask how queer expressions of community at the margins of church and society may serve as guides for churches seeking to cultivate communities of mutual care and support for the isolated and those marginalized in society by forces of oppression and violence. Seriously considering what lessons queer communities can teach communities of faith will necessitate an increased focus upon human situations of suffering and injustice — circumstances similar to those encountered by queer communities throughout the last century.

Here, too, queer examples of community hold the potential to provoke thoughtful action toward the cultivation of communities working toward social change.

Radicals and Reformers: Community as Catalyst for Social Change

Churches and denominations in the United States and around the world are faced with myriad ethical concerns that call for the prophetic voice and engaged activism of faith communities — from LGBTQ rights and inclusion, to immigration, racial justice, prison reform, gross economic disparities, women's rights and equality, human trafficking, and gun violence. But for Christian churches in the United States (especially predominantly white congregations), a comfort of life at the center of the social sphere has often eroded the critical, socially reforming, radical edges that have defined the most important moments in Christian history — moments when churches acted as justice-seeking communities rather than ecclesial props for an unjust status quo.

Given a historic Christian solidarity with the marginalized and a prophetic confrontation of the powerful — as exemplified in the ministry of Jesus, as well as the modern prophetic witness of Christian figures like Walter Rauschenbusch,[27] Dorothy Day,[28] Howard Thurman,[29] Martin Luther King, Jr.,[30] and Desmond Tutu,[31] — Christian communities working as catalysts for social change should be a given. But on the landscape of Christianity in the contemporary Unites States, it is most definitely not. It is often easier for congregations to enjoy the comfortable respectability that comes with numerical majority and the cultural legitimacy of a dominant religious status than to engage in the risky work of prophetic movement toward a more just society. Thus, many opportunities for prophetic engagement are forfeited in an attempt to avoid congregational controversy and preserve a sense of respectability in the eyes of the wider community.

Queer communities as catalysts for social change should also seem obvious. As I argued in the Preface, queer is a term of radical resistance. Queer stands in disruption to the ways we catalogue people based upon the embodiment of difference and the dynamics of power and privilege attached to these identity categories. Queer should disturb our perception enough to question the taken-for-granted and imagine life beyond the dictates of the status quo. But today, LGBTQ people often fall short of this radical, revolutionary, queer identity. For as much rhetorical negativity that is expressed toward a perceived gay agenda, the docket has actually become quite tame. Gay marriage occupies much of our time and energy, with faith groups and political organizations centered on gaining parity for same-sex couples in the rights, benefits, and protections that heterosexual couples enjoy through the legal bonds of matrimony.

But in the history of queer community formation, queer people have often come together to form dynamic expressions of community as catalysts for social change. Beyond a simple example of community as catalyst for social change, however, the shape of queer communities since the 1950s should alert us to contrasting visions that can divide community action toward social change and the possibilities that exist for greater cooperation — both in churches and in queer community organizing. One primary division is that which perennially arises between radical and reforming views of social change.

Radicals — those working to subvert the maintenance of an oppressive status quo and to overturn the operations of freedom-curtailing institutions — often hold rather negative views of reformers. Radicals — often seen staging protests and pickets, dramatically drawing public attention to social ills, practicing nonviolent civil disobedience — sometimes see reformers as tepid in their fervor for justice and deem their lackluster methods ineffectual in bringing about real change. In contrast to radicals, reformers more often work within institutions to change them, rather than outside to challenge them. Reformers see oppression at work in institutions they love, and they strive to reshape and change these institutions into more just forms.

But reformers often take a negative view of radicals, too. Reformers — often seen pouring over bylaws and parliamentary procedures, more at home in a board meeting than on a picket line, employing less publicly visible strategies toward social change — can see their radical neighbors as impatient rabble-rousers, lacking an understanding of how the real world works. Reformers believe that if only radicals would allow the process to work, justice could be realized and institutions changed for the better. Instead, radicals may come to view problems as too deep and widespread for any tame process of change to achieve its intended effects.[32]

Tensions between radicals and reformers have existed throughout Christian history, as well as through the history of queer activism. These tensions have also arisen in the legacy of feminist struggles for women's rights[33] and the civil rights work of African Americans.[34] But radicalism and reformation can — and probably should — comingle much more often than they do in our striving for social change. Our rendering of history, however, doesn't often afford us the point of view necessary to equally appreciate the work of radicals and reformers. For example, in popular renderings of the gay rights movement, a premium is placed upon the flurry of change that ensued following the Stonewall riots, with less attention given to the mundane reforming work of the Mattachine Society and the Daughters of Bilitis in the decades preceding Stonewall or the highly organized (and eventually, politically savvy) AIDS activism in the decades following Stonewall.

D'Emilio even argues that the reason a police raid on the Stonewall Inn in 1969 was experienced by patrons as a riot-sparking affront was due in large part to the success of gay groups working with the city government and State Liquor Authority to diminish the once commonplace police harassment of gay establishments.[35] Without this background of slow reformation of police practices, the commonplace raid of yet another gay bar in a long history of gay bar raids may never have sparked the radical activism of a new generation of queer communities.

We should not presume that the only difference between radicals and reformers is a difference in strategy. There are sometimes important differences in theory, too. For example, early groups like the Daughters of Bilitis and Mattachine pursued a rather conservative program of accommodating themselves to society by working closely with profession-als (sociologists, psychologists, etc.) who could provide a "respectable" public voice to a group of publicly despised gays and lesbians. In con-trast, other groups — and even some individuals within these groups — believed that the social status quo was too broken for mere accom-modation to hold any promise of a better life for queer people. Rather, radical groups expressed "opposition to the culturally dominant view of same-sex eroticism and rejected the notion that anyone other than gay men and women possessed the authority to make judgments about homosexuality."[36] Instead of accommodation, they challenged gays and lesbians, as well as a larger public, to question a simple acceptance of the status quo. They demanded that their own voices be heard and not through the mouthpiece of "respectable" professionals.

To be clear, these divisions did not exist between those who desired social change and those who didn't. They are differences that existed among those who were hard at work to bring about a more just and less violent society for queer people. With the hindsight of history, one lesson suggested by the diverse perspectives of queer people forming communities as catalysts for social changes is this: Without the work of the reformers, the stage wouldn't have been appropriately set for the radi-cals, and without the radicals, the slow tilling of the soil by the reformers may never have reaped the harvest of greater justice. But the differing visions and strategies between these groups often meant that they failed to work in cooperation. Reformers were often motivated by a desire to slowly, quietly, gradually change the present reality toward a more just accommodation of those who are marginalized. In contrast, radicals were propelled by a utopic vision of the future to be ushered in swiftly through more vocal and direct action.

It is between the present reality and the utopic, eschatological vision of a more just future that churches, too, must undertake our work toward the increase of justice and the decrease of violence. Melding a radical vision with reforming work requires the blending of prophetic

vision and pragmatic action, a balance of speed and expedience in cultivating a more just reality.

The impatience queer radicals expressed toward the more gradual work of gay and lesbian reformation should remind us that with the
good work of reformation comes the potential to gradually forget a more
radical vision through increased comfort with the status quo. Thus, the
work of reformation must always be infused with a more radical critique
of the status quo and an inspired eschatological vision of a more just
future. In other words, we must hold a critical awareness that our works
of reformation will always fall short. Here we might be reminded of
one of the tenants of the Protestant Reformation, *semper reformanda* —
"always to be reformed." Reformation is always incomplete; it must be
goaded ever forward by a more radical vision and persistence in enacting
change. Likewise, while radical action is often extraordinarily successful,
it is unsustainable for lengthy periods and must be joined by the expedience of the long, prodding, pragmatic activity of reformation.

In our churches' work toward justice on a multitude of ethical
concerns, radicals need reformers and reformers need radicals. While the
greatest possibility for change seems to emerge from the work of radicals
— those who present a vision of the future set in stark relief from the
status quo and who persist in direct action to bring that future about —
it also appears that the success of radicals would be rendered impossible
if not for the slow, plodding work that reformers undertake for years in
advance and continue long after the effects of brief-but-profound bursts
of radicalism begin to wane. Radical, direct, confrontational practices are
only effective for so long and often only in short bursts of concentrated
energy. Eventually, reforming practice must continue its step-by-step, lit-
tle-by-little movement, even when the results aren't nearly as impressive
or achievable in the brief timespan as those of radical action.

Churches can learn a great deal from this history of queer community organizing for social change. We must not make the mistake of
so many before us — dismissing the radicals among us because their
heads seem to be in the clouds with visions of justice that others cannot

yet imagine. These radicals have glimpsed the eschatological vision of a world yet to come where justice rolls down like waters. Their dreams must inspire us. But we must also avoid the pitfalls of radical impatience with those who choose to work from within — leveraging the weight of institutions in tipping the scales of justice in favor of the marginalized. These reformers are living lessons in tenacity. Their labor should rouse our commitment.

Differences within communities working as catalysts for social change should also point to the reality that within every community there is a great deal of diversity and difference. Just as there is no monolithic "LGBTQ Community" of single mind and purpose, so too there is no monolithic "Christian Community," as evidenced by a vast diversity of denominations and religious organizations and the great deal of difference represented within each of these groups. This realization should help us to question the role of unity within our formations of community.

Questioning the "Unity" of Community: Christian and Queer

When I overhear anyone begin a sentence with the words, "Christians believe . . . ," I cringe. More often than not, what follows is a statement of Christian doctrine that, as a Christian minister, I don't believe. Likewise, when I overhear someone begin a sentence with, "Well, in the LGBT community . . . ," I hold my breath. Whatever descriptor follows usually causes me to wonder, as a "member" of that supposed community, if perhaps I was absent from the meeting where the detail in question was decided.

While I do not believe in the existence of *the* LGBT Community (singular and with a capital C) — which presumes some monolithic unity of mind and purpose — I have experienced and witnessed myriad examples of queer communities (plural and with a lowercase "c"). These expressions of togetherness, love, care, and purposeful activity toward social change can serve as examples of relationship-in-community for all of us. Queer people have much to teach churches about the formation of community at the margins — communities that are sources of mutual care and that wage important struggles for the prophetic reform of an oppressive status quo.

These are lessons churches are often in desperate need of learning in an era of comfortable Christianity — an era when Christianity is often equated with exclusivity rather than inclusivity, closed-mindedness rather than openness to the Spirit of God, judgment rather than mercy. The limits of Christian community are often easily discernable from those who look on from the outside, as well as those on the margins within faith communities.

But queer people haven't always gotten it right, either. I have also experienced the limits of queer communities in ways that call into question the role of unity within any community. It is important for churches to learn lessons alongside queer people from the many examples of queer community that fall far short of the ideal. These lessons on community are sometimes easier to learn from another group's example, and queer people must be willing to teach churches the ways we've gotten it wrong alongside the many ways we've gotten it right.

I remember being at a party once where several volunteers and employees of a local LGBTQ community center were talking. Overhearing a conversation about a recent event at the center, a white gay man and paid employee in leadership at the center referred to a bisexual woman who volunteers at center events, saying, "I don't even know why she volunteers. She isn't really even gay." In my shock at this explicit prejudicial attitude toward a bisexual person, I had to come to terms with the fact that LGBTQ communities exist in a complex matrix of boundaries and divisions that serve to include and exclude based upon varied markers of identity. In our inclusive work, we often overlook the various ways we require others to downplay or erase important differences in order to be included in our communities and movements.

For example, at a time when queer characters are beginning to emerge on television and film in greater numbers, these portrayals are often shaped around dominant racial and class statuses — white gay men who are highly educated with ample expendable income. While even this demographic contains within it a vast array of difference, the caricature is telling. It should concern us when the only representations of sexual difference that seem permissible in the media are characters that embody a dominant racial and gender identification and a privileged class status.[37] These portrayals are obviously not representative of the vast differences that exist among queer people in the larger society, somehow deemed unfit as public images of queer people. But the fictional accounts of queer life aren't the only problem.

Communities formed by queer people have often fallen far short of the ideals of diversity and inclusion espoused by queer organizations.[38] One key example is racism embedded within queer community organizing. Keith Boykin argues, "Black lesbians and gays have been tokenized, ignored, or simply patronized while the predominantly white gay and lesbian community has defined values, issues, agendas, and symbols without meaningful black contribution."[39] When black queer people have been included in gay rights movements, the inclusion is often forged through paternalistic dynamics by which they aren't afforded the respect of individuals with important perspectives and meaningful responsibilities. Lesbians have persistently challenged the sexism harbored within male-dominated gay movements[40] from early strife between members of the Daughters of Bilitis and Mattachine to the contemporary experiences conveyed by Urvashi Vaid about the attitudes she faced in her work as the Executive Director of the National Gay and Lesbian Task Force.[41] D'Emilio describes the classism expressed by the leadership of Mattachine and the Daughters of Bilitis in "attempting to isolate the 'deviant' members of the gay community from its 'respectable' middle-class elements."[42] So too, bisexual and transgender people are regularly forgotten, overlooked or devalued within LGBTQ communities — evidence of the monosexism and transphobia alive within LGBTQ collectives. The differences within and among queer communities are regularly minimized in favor of queer representations that reflect the embodiment of racial, gender, and class privilege.

This calls into question the limits of unity within expressions of queer community and should give churches pause to consider the limits of unity in Christian communities, as well. The unity of faith communities, too, has its limits; boundaries circumscribing inclusion into community are drawn along many different lines — racial identity, class status, sexual orientation or gender identity, and, of course, doctrinal conformity. It is also the case that many expressions of Christian community are formed at the expense of denying difference within the community. I think, for example, of congregations I've encountered that tout a wide diversity of cultural, racial, and international representation among congregants, only to discover that the worship service and prevailing community mores are reminiscent of white congregations from the 1950s. The congregation's diversity exists in name only, visible only through visual representation but entirely absent from meaningful expression and influence in the shaping of community life. We must be persistent in asking, "When we tout the ideal of unity within our communities, is this simply a polite code word for uniformity — the feigning of unity through the denial of difference that exists within and among us?"

In our excitement to celebrate the diversity among us, we should be critically aware of those differences that are not represented within our communities. Beyond mere representation, we should be careful to ask how even community members are subtly required to deny, diminish, or erase certain expressions of difference — whether in race, class, gender, ability, or sexuality — in order to fit in and enjoy the benefits of inclusion in community. In order to take the guesswork out of the equation so that no one has to wonder if these difference-denying dynamics exist within their communities, we should simply assume that they always do exist in some form — requiring the denial and erasure of difference in ways that may escape our awareness.

Simple inclusion of others into community is actually very easy work, as it often places the burden upon those being included to look like and act like suitable community members. But the unity of even the most inclusive communities has limits and they're usually not too difficult to discover. Queer communities, Christian communities, and queer Christian communities alike must be willing to question the ideals of unity, inclusion, and diversity. We must ask: What are the ideals that we wish to guide our community formation? Perhaps unity, inclusion, and diversity are not enough.

Instead, we may move beyond the mere representation of difference within our communities to a privileging of difference. To privilege embodiments of difference is to commit to having our community life shaped and changed by different others. Beyond the inclusion of others, privileging difference means learning from others. Indeed, the privileging of difference is at the heart of this book's message, seeking to learn from different others in ways that enrich the lives of all. Privileging difference is a stance of respectful, compassionate curiosity into the lives and experiences of those who differ from the dominant norm — whether in race, gender, sexual orientation, religion, nationality, or otherwise. Beyond celebrating the diversity of our communities, privileging difference means having our communities shaped and changed through the influence of different others.

Forming community with intentionality and care is a lot of work. If your church hasn't already discovered this, then you're probably missing out on the best parts of life in community. In an era when churches must become even more intentional about the formation of community — when regular involvement in a congregation is no longer a given for a majority of the U.S. population and confidence in faith communities is regularly shaken by scandal — queer examples of community as life-sustaining source of mutual care and justice-seeking catalyst for social change hold a great deal of potential to inform the work of congregations.

Queer communities serve as inspiring examples of the potential for community to address the isolation that overwhelms so many lives.

They are authentic examples of community as source of mutual care, support, and purposeful action. But queer communities are also repositories of wisdom for congregations and contain within them many queer Christians with the experience to help churches cultivate a rich community life. Within the many congregations that persistently deny the differences of sexual orientation and gender identity that exist in their pews, this erasure of difference becomes especially detrimental. The difference queer people are being required to deny is the very difference that makes us qualified to facilitate the formation of community within the congregations we love so dearly. With the firsthand experience of forming community at the margins of church and society, queer people must now become the church's queer teachers.

Notes

[1] For a thorough history of gay subcultural development in New York City, see George Chauncey, *Gay New York: Gender, Urban Culture, and the Making of the Gay Male World*, 1890-1940 (New York: Basic Books, 1994).

[2] Represented in this section is a *very brief* and *selective* history of gay and lesbian cultural development and rights movements in the U.S., focused primarily upon the mid-20th century. For readers wishing for a more robust portrayal of this history, see Chauncey, *Gay New York*; John D'Emilio, *Sexual Politics, Sexual Communities: The Making of a Homosexual Minority in the United States*, 1940-1970, 2nd ed. (Chicago: University of Chicago Press, 1983); Martin Duberman, *Stonewall* (New York: Dutton, 1993); Urvashi Vaid, *Virtual Equality: The Mainstreaming of Gay & Lesbian Liberation* (New York: Anchor, 1995).

[3] For much earlier historical treatment of homosexuality, see John Boswell, *Christianity, Social Tolerance, and Homosexuality: Gay People in Western Europe from the Beginning of the Christian Era to the Fourteenth Century* (Chicago: University of Chicago Press, 1980).

[4] D'Emilio, *Sexual Politics, Sexual Communities*, 10-11.

[5] D'Emilio, *The World Turned*, 80.

[6]D'Emilio, *Sexual Politics, Sexual Communities*, 17.

[7]D'Emilio, *Sexual Politics, Sexual Communities*, 18.

[8]Kenneth D. Wald, "The Context of Gay Politics," in *The Politics of Gay Rights*, eds. Craig A. Rimmerman, Kenneth D. Wald, and Clyde Wilcox (Chicago: University of Chicago Press, 2000), 9.

[9]Chauncey, *Gay New York*, 173.

[10]Chauncey, *Gay New York*, 337.

[11]D'Emilio, *Sexual Politics, Sexual Communities*, 44.

[12]D'Emilio, *Sexual Politics, Sexual Communities*, 46-51.

[13]D'Emilio, *Sexual Politics, Sexual Communities*, 108.

[14]Keith O. Boykin, "Where Rhetoric Meets Reality: The Role of Black Lesbians and Gays in 'Queer' Politics," in *The Politics of Gay Rights*, eds. Craig A. Rimmerman, Kenneth D. Wald, and Clyde Wilcox (Chicago: University of Chicago Press, 2000), 81.

[15]D'Emilio, *The World Turned*, 13. See also John D'Emilio, *Lost Prophet: The Life and Times of Bayard Rustin* (New York: Free Press, 2003).

[16]D'Emilio, *Sexual Politics, Sexual Communities*, 233.

[17]Vaid, *Virtual Equality*, 294.

[18]Chauncey, *Why Marriage?*, 97.

[19]Vaid, *Virtual Equality*, 79.

[20]John D'Emilio, *The World Turned: Essays on Gay History, Politics, and Culture* (Durham, NC: Duke University Press, 2002), 40

[21]Kathy Rudy, *Sex and the Church: Gender, Homosexuality, and the Transformation of Christian Ethics* (Boston: Beacon Press, 1997), 78.

[22]D'Emilio, *The World Turned*, 96.

[23]D'Emilio, *The World Turned*, 96.

[24]Nicholas Ray, "Lesbian, Gay, Bisexual and Transgender Youth: An Epidemic of Homelessness," National Gay and Lesbian Task Force Policy Institute and the National Coalition for the Homeless (2006): 1-2. Online at: http://www.thetaskforce.org/downloads/reports/reports/HomelessYouth.pdf

[25]Rudy, *Sex and the Church*, 72.

[26]For examples, see The Ali Forney Center in New York City (http://www.aliforneycenter.org), and The Ruth Ellis Center in Highland Park, MI (http://www.ruthelliscenter.org).

[27]See Walter Rauschenbusch, *Christianity and the Social Crisis of the 21st Century: The Classic that Woke Up the Church*, ed. Paul Rauschenbusch (New York: HarperOne, 2007).

[28]See Dorothy Day, *The Long Loneliness: The Autobiography of the Legendary Catholic Social Activist* (New York: HarperCollins, 1952).

[29]See Howard Thurman, *Jesus and the Disinherited* (Boston: Beacon Press, 1976/1996).

[30]See Martin Luther King, Jr., *Strength to Love* (Minneapolis: Fortress Press 1963/2010).

[31]See Desmond Tutu, *No Future Without Forgiveness* (New York: Doubleday, 1999).

[32]An example of this is queer people who do not see the institution of marriage as worth reforming for the accommodation of same-sex couples because the institution itself is too corrupt and tied to patriarchy and relational inequality. For readers interested in this perspective, see Michael Warner, *The Trouble with Normal: Sex, Politics, and the Ethics of Queer Life* (New York: The Free Press, 1999). Another example can be seen in those who believe "prison *reform*" falls too short of the radical changes needed in the American penal system. For readers interested in this perspective, see Angela Y. Davis, *Are Prisons Obsolete?* (New York: Seven Stories Press, 2003).

[33]An important work to consider here is Audre Lorde's famed essay "The Master's Tools Will Never Dismantle the Master's House" in *Sister Outsider* (New York: Ten Speed Press, 1984/2007).

[34]See James H. Cone, *Martin & Malcolm & America: A Dream or a Nightmare* (Maryknoll, NY: Orbis, 1991).

[35]D'Emilio, *The World Turned*, 53.

[36]D'Emilio, *Sexual Politics, Sexual Communities*, 108.

[37]For a discussion of the ways that these stereotyped portrayals of gays and lesbians in the media may actually *exacerbate* the isolation experienced by queer adolescents, see Rob Cover, *Queer Youth Suicide, Culture and Identity: Unliveable Lives?* Burlington, VT: Ashgate, 2012), 134.

[38]For a thorough analysis of these dynamics in relation to race, see Boykin, "Where Rhetoric Meets Reality: The Role of Black Lesbians and Gays in 'Queer' Politics" (cited above); and Darnell L. Moore, "An Interrogation of the Black Presence in the

Queer Project," *Trans-Scripts* 1 (2011): 154-171. For a treatment of racial dynamics in contemporary gay rights activism, see "Divided We Stand: The Racial and Gender Status Quo," in Vaid's *Virtual Equality* (cited above). Of particular interest to churches addressing the intersection of racial and sexual identities is Patrick S. Cheng, *Rainbow Theology: Bridging Race, Sexuality, and Spirit* (New York: Seabury, 2013); Miguel A. De La Torre, *A Lily Among the Thorns: Imagining a New Christian Sexuality* (San Francisco: Wiley, 2007); Kelly Brown Douglas, *Sexuality and the Black Church: A Womanist Perspective* (Maryknoll, NY: Orbis, 1999); Horace L. Griffin, *Their Own Receive Them Not: African American Lesbians & Gays in Black Churches* (Cleveland, OH: Pilgrim, 2006).

[39]Boykin, "Where Rhetoric Meets Reality," 82-3.

[40]Adrienne Rich, "The meaning of our love for women is what we have constantly to expand (1977)," in *Come out Fighting: A Century of Essential Writing on Gay & Lesbian Liberation*, ed. Chris Bull (New York: Thunder's Mouth Press/Nation Books, 2001), 151.

[41]See Vaid, *Virtual Equality*.

[42]D'Emilio, Sexual Politics, *Sexual Communities*, 113

Chapter Three

Lessons on Faithfulness

In an era when U.S. churches and denominations are hemorrhaging members,[1] anyone attempting to beat down the doors to enter our houses of worship should raise our curiosity a bit. Most churches never experience the problem of people fighting their way into the pews on Sunday morning. But in an era when nearly every denomination in the United States is experiencing some degree of decline, churches have tenaciously worked to keep lesbian, gay, bisexual, and transgender people out — excluding openly queer people from membership, baring partnered gay and lesbian persons from pathways to ordination into the clergy, and publicly decrying the danger that queer lives pose to the common good.

Perhaps even more remarkable than queer people forming community at the margins of society or developing loving, committed relationships despite facing social ostracism is the astonishing reality that many queer persons continue to maintain deep personal faith commitments and strong ties to churches.

It is particularly telling that the first building ever owned by a gay organization wasn't a community center or a recreation complex. It wasn't an office building for lobbyists or a facility for activists. It was a church. The first building ever owned by a gay organization was the permanent sanctuary built by the Metropolitan Community Church

(MCC) in the early 1970s. The MCC quickly grew to become the largest LGBT grassroots organization in history.[2]

But the heritage of queer Christian faithfulness is often ignored in contemporary debates on sexuality and gender identity. We fill our Christian discourse on sexuality with questions like, "Can people be both lesbian, gay, bisexual, or transgender and Christian?" and "Should we allow non-celibate queer people to be church members or ordained clergypersons?" All the while, queer Christians daily live out the answer to these questions through the example of their very lives — lives of faithfulness and commitment to Christ amid widespread rejection and violence emanating from faith communities. These dynamics of Christian faithfulness amid "Christian" rejection should cause churches to inquire,

What can we learn from the examples of queer people who maintain strong faith commitments amid widespread rejection by churches?[3]

The possibilities opened by this question move us beyond suspicious questions of "can" and "should," to look both curiously and compassionately at living queer exemplars of Christian faithfulness. The lessons we stand to learn from queer lives of faithfulness are far richer than can be gained by simply congratulating queer people for "sticking with it" despite rejection from their faith communities. Quite frankly, I have grown tired of hearing faith leaders tell their queer members to "stick with it" and "hang in there" as their church or denomination sluggishly addresses its history of queer marginalization and slowly adopts tepid practices of welcome and qualified affirmation. Queer people have far more to teach churches about faithfulness than lessons in persistence amid religiously fueled torment from those who occupy our pulpits and share our pews (though we've had to learn those lessons quite well). The most important lessons on faithfulness come from a careful querying of queer faith experience — the living practice of Christian faith on the margins of established faith communities.

" . . . and I by my works will show you my faith"[4]

Churches have long undertaken the search for evidence that queer people can justifiably call themselves faithful Christians, too. Much of this evidentiary probing is centered on "what the Bible says about homosexuality." These discussions often occur in the abstract, relying upon biblical or theological evidence to justify whether or not queer people could actually be faithful Christians. And while parsing the words of scripture and deliberating the theological meaning of biblical texts can be important work, most of this inquiry is performed without ever examining the evidence of Christian faithfulness demonstrated in queer lives — presumably a source of some rather biblical evidence of faith.[5]

Same-gender-loving people have practiced Christian faithfulness at the margins of churches for centuries.[6] But these demonstrations of queer faithfulness became more clearly visible in 1946, when several gay members of a Catholic parish in Atlanta, Georgia, were denied participation in the Eucharist, as the priest who had heard their confession of homosexuality passed them by at the altar rail week after week after week. This was not the first time queer Christians were denied access to the Table of the Lord, barred from receiving the elements of communion and the sustenance of community by guardians of the ecclesial status quo. But this time those excluded mounted an audacious, faith-filled response. Renting space in a hotel lounge with a makeshift altar constructed from cocktail tables, a small group of faithful formed a new congregation under the pastoral leadership of George Hyde that eventually took the name Eucharistic Catholic Church — a reminder of the sacrament once, but never again, denied them.[7]

Decades later, another minister with a history of anguished soul searching and, at times, outright despair (a spiritual experience reminiscent of so many saints in the Christian tradition), came to understand his call not to divorce his sexuality from his Christian faith but to vocation as an openly gay pastor, ministering with gays and lesbians marginalized by their faith communities. Troy Perry, a Pentecostal minister, gathered twelve people in the living room of his Los Angeles home on October 6,

1968, for the first service of worship for what would grow to become the Metropolitan Community Church.[8] As mentioned above, the MCC — founded months before the famed Stonewall Riots that sparked so much queer activism — would grow to become the largest grassroots movement in LGBT history.

While the MCC provided an alternative space for worship outside the dictates of the exclusionary churches from which its initial members often came, another group began to work from within their tradition to open space for the queer faithful to worship more freely. As MCC became the largest LGBT grassroots organization, Dignity would emerge as the first effort of queer organizing within a particular tradition — in this case, that tradition was the Roman Catholic Church.[9] Dignity groups met on Saturdays instead of Sundays so that members could continue worshipping in their local parishes[10] while benefiting from the combination of theological discussion, group therapy, and Mass offered at Dignity gatherings. Its founder, Father Patrick X. Nidorf — an Augustinian priest and counselor concerned for the wellbeing of gay Catholics — was eventually barred by his superiors from continuing his ministry with gay Catholics, turning leadership of the organization over to its many lay members.[11]

In a cultural climate that makes nominal identification with the Christian faith fairly easy, what can we learn from those who have had no easy time maintaining connection to Christian faith communities? In a contemporary era when it is far easier to exit the four walls of the church in frustration to join the ranks of the spiritual-but-not-religious,[12] what can churches learn from their queer Christian sojourners — modern exemplars of a historic spirit of Christian reformation — who have been unafraid to get their hands dirty cultivating change in the churches and denominations for which they care so deeply?

What should intrigue churches wishing to learn from the history of queer faithfulness is not that these new churches and reform movements were founded, but how they took shape around a set of commitments that aimed to correct the exclusionary practices of Christian community that queer Christians had experienced in their churches. None of these three movements understood their work as creating an exclusively "gay church" for members rejected in other worshipping bodies. But out of their queer histories with Christian churches, each movement embodied in its common life the commitments forged from collective faith experiences of grievous exclusion and anguished marginalization from the Christian communities of their upbringings. And their practice of expansive inclusion extends beyond queer identified Christians.

In the 1940s, the Eucharistic Catholic Church not only provided the first explicitly welcoming religious space for queer worshippers, but they also broke with other exclusionary social norms of the day, forming a racially integrated community of both queer and straight members who transcended denominational divisions.[13] Troy Perry, too, envisioned the MCC becoming a Christian community of broad inclusion. Commenting on Perry, Mark Jordan explains, "Having suffered such bitter exclusion from churches, he was not about to establish a new church on the basis of a reversed exclusion. Given his background, he could never conceive church as anything other than intrinsically expansive."[14] While the majority of early MCC members came from mainline Protestant churches, a quarter were Roman Catholic in heritage, some joined MCC from the Church of Jesus Christ of Latter-day Saints, and still others joined as "friends" — a category of membership that included Jews, agnostics, atheists, and Buddhists who could not align themselves with historic tenets of Christian faith, but who were woven into the fabric of this expansive community.[15]

These faithful, queer Christians refused to be resigned to complacency when faced with the cordoning off of God's expansive table of grace. Their actions bring to mind the challenging words of theologian M. Shawn Copeland when she writes in her book, *Enfleshing Freedom*,

> If my sister or brother is not at the table, we are not the flesh of Christ. If my sister's mark of sexuality must be obscured, if my brother's mark of race must be disguised,

if my sister's mark of culture must be repressed, then
we are not the flesh of Christ. For, it is through and
in Christ's own flesh that the 'other' is my sister, is my
brother; indeed, the 'other' is me.[16]

These faithful, queer reformers were the first to cultivate spaces
for worship that embraced queer bodies as integral parts of the spacious
Body of Christ. In their early ministry, churches that pay close, compassionate attention may catch a glimpse of an expansive practice of
Christian faith often obstructed from view by a Christian heritage punc-
tuated by practices that work to obscure, disguise, and repress markers
of human difference before issuing an invitation to Christian community. But ending the story with these narratives of brave prophetic reform
fails to attend to the equally important expressions of faithfulness in the
myriad lives of queer individuals facing dilemmas of faithfulness unimaginable to most straight, gender-conforming Christians.

"...work out your own salvation with fear and trembling"[17]

Queer Christians are often forced to make some impossibly difficult choices in the life of faith. Queer Christians are regularly asked
to decide between commitment to the communities of faith they love
and pursuing a life free from hiding and shame, blessing the fullness of
their experience as lesbian, gay, bisexual, or transgender people. These
dilemmas of queer Christian faithfulness are difficult to explain in the
abstract. Words like "tension," "distress," and "crisis" are not quite evoca-
tive enough to capture the complex faith experiences of so many queer
Christians who have faithfully worked out their own salvation with fear
and trembling. Take a look at just a few excerpts of first-person accounts
from the book, *Crisis: 40 Stories Revealing the Personal, Social, and
Religious Pain and Trauma of Growing Up Gay in America*:

I could no longer be anything other than who I was. I left my family and also the church. It felt like I was giving up everything that had grounded me since birth. It caused great pain for my family.[18]

Of course, both my parents felt pressured by the church's way of dealing with any kind of dissention — excommunication. And that's essentially what happened to me. Family and friends were not even supposed to associate with me.[19]

There was no language that I knew to describe my sense of alienation. I knew for sure that my secret meant disgrace, if not rejection from family, friends, and community. Fortunately, at age ten, I didn't fully understand that my secret — the sense that I was different from other boys — was punishable by death according to the Bible, Leviticus 20:13. However, I did understand that it was something that put me beyond the pale, beyond the margins, with no hope of moving toward the center.[20]

With the stereotypical rabidity of a Southern country preacher, my pastor condemned gay and lesbian people from the pulpit almost every Sunday . . . How does an eleven- or twelve-year-old "preacher boy" with a promising future in the church — one who has already gained the respect of being called brother — come out as the very thing so hated and condemned by the people he loves and cherishes as family?[21]

Feeling exhausted by my attempts to hide my secret and keep up my reputation as a "good Christian," I began to spiral into depression. I was lonely and hurting. The church leaders I talked to . . . encouraged me to keep fighting it. They said Jesus would heal my sin and that He would fix me if only I stayed faithful.[22]

While queer Christians have, indeed, had to work out their salvation with "fear and trembling," as described in the words from Philippians quoted in the heading above, it is the persistence of queer people in believing the words of the subsequent verse that is most remarkable: "for it is God who is at work in you . . . " (2:13). The ability to continue to practice one's faith and to trust in God's love — despite having very little, if any, demonstration of this Divine love from the churches and communities of faith that nurtured you — is a remarkable demonstration of faithfulness lived out in so many lives. This faithfulness points beyond the persistence of queer Christians, staying within their churches and denominations to work for change, to a deep and abiding faithfulness to the gospel message of God's expansive love.

Understandably, some queer people must walk away from churches forever. For their own psychological and spiritual wellbeing — to save their lives and souls — many queer people find it necessary to disavow all symbols of the faith that has been used as a weapon against them. But while churches have so often failed to act as the mouthpiece of God's love for queer people, many queer faithful have often taken up their mantle as subversive prophets of love and bold practitioners of justice.

So, while debates over the nuances of biblical interpretation surrounding homosexuality can be important undertakings, for sure, it is coming to seem that many of our ongoing debates are little more than pious prattling in the face of so many queer Christian lives lived as demonstrations of a tenacious and untiring Christian faithfulness that is in short supply in U.S. churches. How, then, might churches learn something of importance from these queer examples of faithfulness? In a social context that makes it so easy to disavow the need for connection to faith communities, how can queer Christians who have remained within Christian churches to practice their faith and tenaciously work toward much needed reform become teachers to us all? In short, what can we learn from queer people about what it means to be Christian?

Remember Your Baptism and Be Thankful

As should be clear by now, the questions that often focus our congregational dialogue on Christian faith, sexual orientation and gender identity are not just about queer persons "out there," but queer persons in our midst. Queer Christians haven't been waiting around for an official proclamation of their acceptability before joining in the worship and work of faith communities. Queer people serve churches in every capacity imaginable, even when sometimes having to hide important parts of their lives to escape the scorn of their fellow church members. One critical lesson churches might learn from those queer souls who faithfully remain within the myriad Christian congregations and denominations that so often insist upon their queer Christian illegitimacy, is a lesson about baptismal identity. In an era when many Christian churches struggle to discern and communicate their relevance to an increasingly non-religious society that struggles to see it, the queer faithful seem to know something about the significance of a baptismal identity to which churches should pay close attention.

Traditional debates over queer lives hinge upon the importance of one's sexual orientation or gender identity in delimiting the boundaries of Christian faithfulness. The orientation of one's sexual attraction and the experience and expression of one's gender identity have become key (sometimes appearing as *the* key) for many churches in determining the ability of a person to live in Christian faithfulness. But queer Christians challenge the centrality of one's sexual or gender identity as fundamental to Christian faithfulness by foregrounding, instead, the supremacy of one's baptismal identity. While churches cling to the socially delineated privilege built up around heterosexuality and male/female gender conformity as defining features of Christian character, queer lives of faithfulness serve as reminders to churches that — in Elizabeth Stuart's words — "The baptized belong to another world." Stuart continues,

> To be baptized is to be caught up in a kingdom that does not yet fully exist, that is in the process of becoming; it is to be caught up in the redemption of this world. It is not that the baptized are called to live beyond culture, but that they are called to transform culture by living in it in such a way as to testify to the other world being born within it.[23]

Living out one's baptismal identity over the identifiers of one's sexual or gender identity doesn't diminish the place of these embodied particularities in one's experience of life and faith. Not erasing other important markers of identity that affect our lives and self-understanding — e.g. race, sexuality, ethnicity, gender, ability — a baptismal identity stands as a marker of covenant between an individual and God, as well as between the individual and all other members of Christ's church. Queer Christians live out the binding, covenantal quality of baptismal identity through their faithful persistence to worship and minister within communities of faith, enacting faithful reform toward a more expansive vision of a "kingdom that does not yet fully exist" — to another world being born.

Far from the passive participants and complacent observers that often pass for "faithful church members" in a culture of comfortable Christianity, queer people have demonstrated an active engagement in the reform of Christian churches. Queer people have also produced important and intriguing works of theology, engaging the intersections of Christian faith, sexuality and gender identity. It is a gift that so many lesbian, gay, bisexual, transgender, and queer Christians give to churches, offering our own bodies — our rich and complex experiences of sexuality and gender identity — as grist for the theological mill. For many queer people throughout history, the theological attention paid to their sexuality and gender identity has been unwanted and often meant subjection to suspicious scrutiny and almost inevitable exclusion from Christian community. But many other queer people have leaned into the questions raised by their own sexual and gendered lives to produce thoughtful and challenging works of theology, many of which are referenced throughout this book.

With the witness of their very lives, queer Christians give testimony to the power of baptismal identity to break down the boundaries that are erected around our human particularities and, instead, give rise to peculiar community. A community forged around baptismal identity is formed not in order to mask our particularities but to give expression to a radical embrace of human difference now soaked in the baptismal waters. Early faithful queer Christians gave witness to the radical nature of a baptismal identity — in the Eucharistic Catholic Church's racial integration in 1940s Atlanta, Georgia, in the resolve of Troy Perry not to practice a reverse exclusion in the creation of a "gay church," extending welcome even to those from other faith traditions and no faith tradition at all who became a part of an expansive vision of community.

While many churches remain embroiled in debate to determine whether or not queer people can also be faithful Christians, queer lives actively extend an invitation to churches to pay careful, compassionate attention to our queer faith. The time has come for queer Christians to become our churches' teachers, if we are only willing to change our questions from the "cans" and "shoulds" of suspicious scrutiny and boundary maintenance, to more important inquiries of compassionate curiosity, asking: "How can learning from the examples of queer Christian faithfulness reinvigorate the lives of our struggling congregations and denominations?" "How have the questions we've grown accustomed to asking about sexual orientation and gender identity caused our churches to lose sight of the centrality of a baptismal identity?" "What questions are queer people asking about the intersections of Christian faith, sexuality, and gender identity that we should all be asking?" Churches may be surprised by the lessons they learn.

Notes

[1]A 2012 Pew study reports that the number of Americans who do not identify with any religion is growing at a rapid pace, with one fifth of all Americans and one third of adults under the age of 30 reporting a religiously unaffiliated status. See The Pew Forum on Religion & Public Life, *"Nones" on the Rise: One-in-Five Adults Have No Religious Affiliation* (Washington, DC: Pew Research Center, 2012) accessed March 22, 2013, http://www.pewforum.org/uploadedFiles/Topics/Religious_Affiliation/Unaffiliated/NonesOnTheRise-full.pdf.

[2]George Chauncey, *Why Marriage? The History Shaping Today's Debate Over Gay Equality* (New York: Basic Books, 2004), 91-92.

[3]Asking what churches can learn, through example, about the practice of Christian *faithfulness* from queer people is different from asking what churches can learn about *theology* from the work of LGBT and queer theologians. Both questions are important and, while I intend this chapter to address only the first, readers interested in learning from the work of LGBT and queer theologians may find a helpful starting place in Patrick S. Cheng, *Radical Love: An Introduction to Queer Theology* (New York: Seabury, 2011) and *From Sin to Amazing Grace: Discovering the Queer Christ* (New York: Seabury, 2012) and Elizabeth Stuart, *Gay and Lesbian Theologies: Repetitions with Critical Difference* (Burlington, VT: Ashgate, 2003).

[4]James 2:18

[5]For readers interested in first-person narratives of LGBTQ persons whose lives variously intersect Christian faith, see L. William Countryman and M. R. Ritley, *Gifted by Otherness: Gay and Lesbian Christians in the Church* (New York: Morehouse, 2001); Mitchell Gold and Mindy Drucker, eds., *Crisis: 40 Stories Revealing the Personal, Social, and Religious Pain and Trauma of Growing Up Gay in America* (Austin, TX: Greenleaf, 2008); Cody J. Sanders, ed., *Rightly Dividing the Word of Truth: A Resource for Congregations in Dialogue on Sexual Orientation and Gender Identity*, 2nd ed. (Charlotte, NC: Baptist Peace Fellowship of North America, 2013); and Leanne McCall Tigert and Timothy Brown, eds., *Coming Out Young and Faithful* (Cleveland, OH: Pilgrim, 2001).

[6]For this history, see John Boswell, *Christianity, Social Tolerance, and Homosexuality: Gay People in Western Europe from the Beginning of the Christian Era to the Fourteenth Century* (Chicago: University of Chicago Press, 1980).

[7]Heather Rachelle White, "Proclaiming Liberation: The Historical Roots of LGBT Religious Organizing, 1946-1976," *Nova Religio: The Journal of Alternative and Emergent Religions* 11(4) (2008): 103-4.

[8]Mark D. Jordan, *Recruiting Young Love: How Christians Talk About Homosexuality* (Chicago: University of Chicago Press, 2011), 119.

[9]Jordan, *Recruiting Young Love*, 113.

[10]Jordan, *Recruiting Young Love*, 121.

[11]White, "Proclaiming Liberation," 111.

[12]The same Pew study cited above shows that of the 46 million religiously unaffiliated adults in the U.S., many continue to consider themselves religious or spiritual in ways that are not evidenced by formal religious affiliation with 68% reporting belief in God and 37% identifying as "spiritual" but not "religious." Pew Forum, *"Nones" on the Rise*, 9-10.

[13]Jordan, *Recruiting Young Love*, 70.

[14]Jordan, *Recruiting Young Love*, 119.

[15]White, "Proclaiming Liberation," 109.

[16]M. Shawn Copeland, *Enfleshing Freedom: Body, Race, and Being* (Minneapolis, MN: Fortress, 2009), 82.

[17]Philippians 2:12

[18]Bruce Bastian, in *Crisis: 40 Stories Revealing the Personal, Social, and Religious Pain and Trauma of Growing Up Gay in America*, ed. Mitchell Gold and Mindy Drucker (Austin, TX: Greenleaf, 2008), 34.

[19]H. Alexander Robinson, in *Crisis*, 41.

[20]Rodney Powell, in *Crisis*, 54-5.

[21]Matt Comer, in *Crisis*, 70.

[22]Jared Horsford, in *Crisis*, 77.

[23]Elizabeth Stuart, "Sacramental Flesh," in *Queer Theology: Rethinking the Western Body*, ed. Gerard Loughlin (Malden, MA: Blackwell, 2007), 68.

Chapter Four

Lessons on Love

Love seems almost synonymous with the Christian life — at least in the minds of most Christians. Many of the Bible verses we instill in our children when they are growing up in church are about love. For example: "You shall love your neighbor as yourself" (Matthew 22: 39); "This is my commandment, that you love one another as I have loved you" (John 15:12); "And now faith, hope, and love abide, these three; and the greatest of these is love" (1 Corinthians 13:13); "Beloved, let us love one another, because love is from God; everyone who loves is born of God and knows God. Whoever does not love does not know God, for God is love." (1 John 4: 8). This list of passages on love could continue on and on, ranging throughout the Bible. It seems obvious that the theme of love inhabits a central role in Christian theology and ministry.

Love is even a major theme shaping the attitudes of churches toward queer people. And while love seems like a very hopeful attitude for churches to hold in relation to queer lives, there is some difficulty in the way love gets translated into practice. In the day-to-day ministries of Christian churches and parachurch organizations, practices of loving queer people take on vastly different shapes and forms, some with detrimental effects in the lives of queer people.

To be sure, many churches have become well practiced at loving queer people into the life-giving embrace of community. But other churches seem intent on loving queer people to death. While churches regularly espouse the central Christian theme of love in relation to queer people, what these churches presume the term love to mean in practice varies so widely that we have stretched and distorted the term beyond recognition.

Thus, the intersection of queer lives and Christian practices of love serve as a helpful starting place for churches and religious organizations seeking not only to better understand love, but also for those wishing to become intentionally reflective about practices of ministry undertaken in the name of Christian love. With this aim in mind, we can ask:

What can churches learn from the many and varied Christian practices of love experienced — and sometimes endured — by queer people?

Before we can address this question there are a few important matters to which we must attend. Recall in the Introduction, I mentioned that our typical debates over sexuality and gender identity come with a certain arrangement of power that places some in the center and others on the margins of the conversation — some get to do the speaking and others simply get spoken about. Thinking about the ways we are all positioned in conversations and debates over queer lives is vital if we are to become more reflective about our practices of love. This is especially so due to the fact that, for many of these practices, there are clear and discernable divisions between those doing the loving and those who become the objects of Christian love.

Some of the preliminary concerns we must address in order to be reflective about our practices of love for queer people revolve around our social location. This is a term for the varied markers of identity we embody in terms of gender, sexuality, race, class, ethnicity, etc. and the way that these assorted markers of identity locate us in conversations like this one on the meaning and practice of love for queer people. Our social location colors the way we see and experience the world and provides a multifaceted lens through which we view ourselves in relation to others.

In moving us toward a greater understanding of the role that social location plays in addressing religious and theological questions, Kelly Brown Douglas in her book, *Sexuality and the Black Church*, argues,

> If who we are — that is, our life experiences — helps us to determine our theological questions and concerns, then who we are also circumscribes those questions and concerns. Our particular social, historical, cultural, and political actualities can free us to address certain topics, and at other times those very same actualities can hinder us from doing so. Likewise, these life circumstances can assist us in perceiving the meaning of God's revelation, or they can obstruct our view of that revelation.[1]

In other words, she is assisting us in seeing how our particular embodied differences not only shape our responses to questions like the one of love, but they often determine the very questions we ask to begin with.

For example, when we enter a conversation on Christian love for queer people as heterosexual, biological gender-conforming Christians in a congregation seeking to act lovingly toward queer people, we may see the practices of love we develop as a simple outgrowth of the gospel's imperative to love our neighbors. If, however, our social location as queer people positions us on the receiving end of Christian practices of love, we may have an entirely different point of view on these loving practices. Our social location may cause us to question if the practice of love we've been asked to receive should even be called loving at all. Becoming curious about the intersections between queer lives and Christian practices of love holds the potential for helping churches imagine and enact practices of love that are intentionally reflective and cognizant of how these practices are experienced by their intended recipients.

There are three preliminary questions we should consider when attempting to understand how churches practice love for queer people. Every practice of love toward queer people holds within it an answer to these three interrelated questions, even when these answers operate behind the scenes of the practices — never explicitly spoken or acknowledged:

- First, "What does it mean to be a sexual human being in relation to God?"

- Second, "How does this understanding obligate churches to act toward queer people?"

- Third, "What practices of ministry align with our understanding of sexual human beings in relation to God and how we feel obligated to respond to queer people?"[2]

Even when these questions have not been openly addressed, one can work backwards by looking at the practice of love itself and asking, "What would a church have to believe about the meaning of sexual human beings in relation to God and how this view obligates churches to act in relation to queer people in order for this practice to seem loving?" It may seem like a complicated process just to understand how to practice something as seemingly simple as love. But it will soon become clear how varied practices of love toward queer people answer these three questions in vastly different ways, bringing about stark contrasts in the way love is expressed by churches and experienced by queer people.

Here, I will explore three broad ways of categorizing the types of love that are currently practiced by churches in relation to queer lives. Each of these types — "normalizing love," "affirming love," and "just love" — lead to particular practices of ministry I have termed "assimilationist," "accommodating," and "adaptive." I will explore how churches have responded to each of the three above questions in order to arrive upon one of these views of love and the practices of ministry that take shape out of that view. I will also make clear throughout how these considerations are not just limited to churches' practices of love in relation to queer people, but also offer to teach us something about the myriad intersections of Christian ministry and the embodiment of human difference.

Normalizing Love & Assimilationist Ministry

Many congregations ask the question, "What does it mean to be a sexual human being in relation to God?" without giving much attention to how our social location determines the way we explore this question. For most churches, this question has been addressed strictly from the perspective of those who identify as heterosexual and biologically gender conforming. If we assume that everyone else simply sees the world and experiences life "like we do," then it is easy to respond to this question without ever seeking out the voices of others who differ from us in sexual or gender identity. The way we read the Bible, the way we understand God, and the way we experience sexuality and gender identity are the norms by which we judge what it means to be a sexual human being in relation to God.

Still others seek to hear the voices of those who differ from the norm of sexual orientation and gender identity, but do not question the arrangement of power that sets heterosexual and gender conforming experience above experiences of difference. For example, heterosexuality and male/female biological gender conformity stand as the unquestioned norm by which all other experiences are judged and assessed, even when we invite those voices of difference into the conversation. Even the offering of an invitation itself illuminates who holds the privileged position in the conversational arrangement!

Whether we simply exclude the experience of sexual and gender difference or assess these differing embodied experiences from the perspective of an unquestioned (and perhaps unquestionable) norm, conducting our inquiry in these ways leads many churches to respond by saying, "According to our understanding, being a sexual human being in relation to God means a clear dichotomous distinction between male and female genders and the expression of sexuality only between one man and one woman."

But then we must explain the experiences of sexual orientation and gender identities that differ from the heterosexual and gender conforming norm. Typically, a first line of explanation relies upon Christian theological concepts like sin. Here, sin typically means some form of deviance from the design of God regarding the experience of gender identity and sexual orientation.[3] Viewing queer people as sinful is then supported by biblical and theological arguments that are typically arrived upon through readings of the Bible and Christian tradition from the vantage point of those at the center of the conversation (i.e., heterosexual persons).[4]

While sin is often the first line of explanation, many churches trying to explain sexual and gender deviations from a presumed divinely-established norm draw upon resources from the sciences as explanatory tools. For instance, many churches and Christian organizations have relied upon psychological explanations to add further support to their notions of the sinfulness exhibited by lesbian, gay, bisexual, and transgender people by adding a supposed scientific layer of sickness on top of the religious explanation of sinfulness.[5] For example, until 1973, homosexuality was considered a mental disorder by the diagnostic criteria of the American Psychiatric Association. This added scientific weight to the credibility of religious rhetoric that portrayed homosexuality as a deviation from the divinely-ordained norm for sexual experience and expression.

With sin and sickness firmly rooting churches' view of queer people as deviant from the divinely-ordained norm, there is a third layer often added to the religious and the scientific explanations: the law.[6] Legal discourse is used less to explain deviance and more to socially enforce the perspectives perpetuated by the religious and psychological discourses. Historian George Chauncey explains the gravity of this legal/psychological intertwining for queer lives, saying,

Fifty years ago, more than half of the nation's states, including New York, Michigan, and California, enacted laws authorizing the police to force persons who were convicted of certain sexual offences, including sodomy — or, in some states, merely suspected of being "sexual deviants" — to undergo psychiatric examinations. Many of these laws authorized the indefinite confinement of homosexuals in mental institutions, from which they were to be released only if they were cured of their homosexuality, something prison doctors soon began to complain was impossible.[7]

But queer people were certainly not the first to experience the perverse intertwining of religious, psychological, and legal discourses to explain and control the "deviance" of those differing from the social norm. It may be helpful to illustrate this intertwining of religious, scientific, and legal discourses with a historical example further removed from the present. In 1851, the physician Samuel Cartwright "discovered" a disease uniquely experienced by African Americans called "drapetomania." This illness manifested itself in a slave's attempt to escape from his white master.[8] Thus, not only did white preachers justify slavery as divinely ordained and based upon the so-called biblical meaning of racial difference,[9] any deviation from this oppressive social arrangement was explained as an illness that must be treated — in this case through whipping and increased surveillance.

Once we come to explain difference as deviance, the second question moves churches from considering the meaning of our sexual lives in relation to God to then ask, "How does this understanding of sexual human beings obligate us to act toward queer people?" Churches and religious organizations range from outright hatred and rejection — seen, for example, in the explicit anti-gay messages of groups like the infamous Westboro Baptist Church of Topeka, Kansas — to practices aimed at helping those who deviate from the norm better fit the presumed divine design for sexual orientation and gender identity. I call these assimilationist practices of ministry.

Assimilationist practices of ministry aim to lovingly aid those who deviate from the norm (in this case, queer people) by fixing, repairing, or healing whatever causes them to stray from the norm.[10] This motivation is what I am calling normalizing love. If a church answers the question, "What does it mean to be a sexual human being in relation to God?" by stating that the divinely-sanctioned norm is a heterosexual sexuality and a gender identity that conforms to a strict biologically-determined male/female binary, then this theological point of view obligates churches to help those who do not fit this design to assimilate, adjust, or conform to the norm. This attitude might be expressed by the phrase, "We love you enough to help you change."

Current examples of these practices are ministries that operate under the names "reparative" or "conversion therapy" and "ex-gay ministries." This type of assimilationist ministry flowing from an attitude of normalizing love for queer people is perhaps best typified by the organization, Exodus International. The annual conference hosted by Exodus is illustrative of the central role love plays in its mission. The Exodus conference is titled "Love Won Out" and aims to equip attendees "to minister in truth and compassion to a loved one who deals with same-sex attractions, respond to misinformation in our culture and defend biblical beliefs with grace and understanding."[11] Guided by biblical and theological interpretations that view heterosexuality as the divinely-sanctioned norm, Exodus practices a ministry of "hope and help to people seeking freedom over their homosexual impulses and behaviors."[12]

In its more psychotherapeutic variety, these assimilationist practices of repair and conversion from homosexual to heterosexual orientation are promoted and defended by the National Association for Research & Therapy of Homosexuality (NARTH). In its psychotherapeutic form, these assimilationist practices striving to repair non-heterosexual orientations and transgender identities are not always strictly tied to Christian motivations of love. Nevertheless, these practices are often adopted and supported by some Christian counselors and organizations that view homosexuality as a deviation from a divinely-sanctioned norm of heterosexuality.[13] Of course, the normalizing variety is but one of the ways churches purport to practice love toward queer people.

Affirming Love & Accommodating Ministry

Many churches and religious organizations have come to see these normalizing practices of love and the accompanying assimilationist practices of ministry as somewhat less than loving, to say the least. In the last few decades, more and more churches and denominations have come to biblical and theological understandings that recognize and celebrate the diversity of God's creation, including the differences of sexual orientation and gender identity witnessed in the lives of lesbian, gay, bisexual, and transgender people.[14] These churches often see the connected patterns in historic, oppressive Christian treatments of women and racial minorities and endeavor to resist replicating the same patterns of religiously-supported injustice and violence against queer people.

Churches holding a more affirming perspective on human difference relating to sexuality and gender identity also draw upon the psychological and social sciences to further bolster their perspectives on queer lives. For example, in protest of practices like reparative therapy and ex-gay ministry, these churches note the overwhelming consensus emerging from the psychological sciences denouncing these practices as harmful to queer lives. From Freud, who said nearly a century ago, "I am . . . of the firm conviction that homosexuals must not be treated as sick people,"[15] to the official statements of the American Psychological Association, the American Psychiatric Association, the American Counseling Association, the American Psychoanalytic Association, the National Association of Social Workers, the National Association of School Psychologists and other organizations representing nearly half-a-million health and mental health professionals, the consensus position of medical and mental health organizations in the twenty-first century is that homosexuality is not a mental disorder and is, therefore, in no need of a cure.[16]

Instead, led by a vision of affirming love, these churches do not view queer people as deviating from a divinely-sanctioned norm of heterosexuality and a male/female biological gender division. Rather than deviant, sinful, or sick, queer people are simply disadvantaged by religious views and social arrangements that marginalize and exclude them from full inclusion into congregations, social institutions like marriage, and family and community embrace. To be sure, some churches holding an attitude of affirming love toward queer people often fall short of putting this love into practice — remaining silent about the matter in order to remain uncontroversial. Many other churches, however, have become quite vocal about their attitude of affirming love for queer lives, putting this love into practice in diverse ways.

So, how does affirming love obligate churches to act in relation to queer people? Led by a theology of love and embrace for the other, LGBTQ persons are accommodated in ways that help them to live more fully into the present structures of church, community, society, etc. The aim of these loving practices is to meet the disadvantaging prejudicial attitudes and exclusionary institutional structures experienced by queer people with loving practices of welcome, affirmation, and inclusion into the life of churches and society at large.

The obligation for action flowing from an attitude of affirming love can be termed accommodating ministry. This perspective on loving ministry is encapsulated in statements from religious organizations steadily working toward the affirmation of queer people. For example, these groups aim toward a "more just, welcoming, and inclusive church, one that welcomes the gifts and graces of all persons, regardless of gender or sexual identity."[17] They assist congregations in making "a public covenant of welcome into their full life and ministry to persons of all sexual orientations, gender identities, and gender expressions."[18] These congregations are ones that are "willing to go on record as welcoming and affirming of all persons without regard to sexual orientation or gender identity. These organizations and individuals have joined together to advocate for the full inclusion of lesbian, gay, bisexual and transgender persons."[19] In more popular and political spheres this stance is often expressed in statements like, "LGBTQ people were born that way, are just as 'normal' as anyone else, and should have the same rights as straight and gender-conforming people."

Accommodating ministry aims to embrace and affirm queer people, leading to practices of love that take the shape of a congregation becoming officially welcoming and affirming of LGBTQ people, performing marriage ceremonies for same-sex couples in the community, and opening pathways to ordination for queer people sensing a call to ministry. In the wider social sphere, accommodating practices take shape around advocacy for the right of same-sex couples to enjoy the benefits, rights, and protections of legal marriage.[20] Accommodating practices of ministry seek to gain equality by creating pathways for access to inclusion in social and ecclesial structures (e.g. marriage, ordination, etc.) that are enjoyed by heterosexual and biologically gender-conforming persons. Through the accommodating practices of ministry flowing from an attitude of affirming love for queer people, many LGBTQ people have come to enjoy ever-greater inclusion into the congregations and denominations that have been their lifetime spiritual homes. Beyond this, the accommodation of queer people has produced many advances in the rights and protections from prejudice that LGBTQ people enjoy in our society, slowly but steadily cultivating a religious and cultural sphere that is increasingly more equitable for queer lives.

Of course, a religious commitment to loving those of gender and sexual difference by accommodating them into the present structures of church and society does not always take the next step toward learning from (rather than simply learning about) gender and sexual difference. This stance often stops short of asking the risky question at the heart of this book, "What do the lives of lesbian, gay, bisexual, transgender, and queer persons have to teach us (all) about God, about faithfulness, about community, about covenant, about love, etc.?" And the even more risky question, "How might the lessons learned from queer lives challenge and change our theologies, communities of faith, and practices of ministry?"

Just Love[21] & Adaptive Ministry

There is at least one more response to the question, "What does it mean to be a sexual human being in relation to God?" This response moves beyond viewing difference as deviance from a divinely-ordained norm and even beyond the perspective that those embodying some difference in sexual orientation or gender identity are simply disadvantaged by social prejudice and in need of acceptance and accommodation into the structures of church and society. From this third perspective, difference in sexual orientation or gender identity isn't just accepted and accommodated, but is highly valued in ways that resist assimilation of embodied difference into the dominant norm. There is, therefore, no need for reparative therapy or ex-gay ministry, because heterosexuality isn't taken as the unquestioned norm for sexual human beingness in relation to God. Likewise, this view compels us to resist simple acts of affirmation when all that results from them are practices of accommodation into present structures of church and society. Instead, embodied difference becomes an important source of creative disturbance that shakes us from becoming overly comfortable with the status quo and leads us to ask new questions and adapt our practices of ministry to ever-changing contexts. Indeed, this view of love is rooted in the example of Jesus whose own life was lived in creative disturbance of the status quo.

Beyond simply accommodating the marginalized into the current structures, this stance seeks to question the status quo in light of the experience of those on the margins. It asks, "If the way things are serves to marginalize some among us, is 'the way things are' the way they have to be?" This is a perspective on the meaning of sexual human beingness in relation to God that views those who differ from the dominant norm as potential teachers, illuminating a pathway toward greater justice for all those pushed to the margins of church and society. This attitude can be termed just love because of its intentional fusion of love for the individuals affected by prejudice and discrimination with a robust understanding and vigorous pursuit of justice in the wider social sphere.

While justice is often a slippery concept to define, I find Iris Marion Young's work helpful in developing a richer understanding of the term. She views the concept of justice extending beyond equality in the material realm of economic capital and possessions. She also sees justice as addressing the freedom and constraint upon one's action, the ability to make decision about one's actions, the ability to develop and exercise one's capacities, and the ability to express one's perspectives on social life.[22] A concept of justice must certainly take into consideration legal concerns, such as the protection from discrimination and harm, the preservation of rights, and equality in access to institutional privileges like marriage. However, a more robust concept of justice must account for the ability of others to experience a sense of freedom in their everyday lives without "institutional conditions which inhibit or prevent people from participating in determining their actions" and place limitations on their ability "to express their feelings and perspectives on social life in contexts where others can listen."[23] This sense of everyday freedom is often what is at stake when considering justice for queer people — especially in the context of faith communities.

Viewing human difference with an attitude of just love leads us to ask questions like these:

- What norms, habits, rules, and symbols do we hold to that keep some among us from being able to openly acknowledge and express their life experience?[24] For example, consider all of the way our religious language and symbols, not to mention our explicit teachings, simply presume that everyone is — or at least should be — heterosexual and identified with their "biologically-assigned" gender. This keeps some from openly expressing experiences of same-sex attraction and love or differing experiences of gender identity. How many of our hymns and liturgies use unnecessarily gendered language? How many of our activities for or sermons about married people presume a heterosexual coupling? How might the arrangement of our physical space (i.e., the division of Sunday school classes, restrooms in church buildings, etc.) presume a strict male/female gender binary?

- Are some forced to hide important details of their life and experience in order to avoid ridicule, exclusion, and possibly violence in order to be a part of our community? For example, what personal consequences might one face if they were to come out as lesbian, gay, bisexual, or transgender within our community of faith? Of those openly queer people in our congregation, what thoughts, feelings, perspectives, and life experiences are kept hidden in order to be seen as acceptable or to fit in? The answer to this question may even surprise congregations that have long been affirming of queer people! Further, must queer people fit into our congregation's norms in every other way (race, socioeconomic class, nationality, etc.) except for their sexual orientation or gender identity in order to experience affirmation and embrace into community?

- Upon whose terms are queer people embraced into our congregation or faith community? For example, I once heard a heterosexually-identified person proudly congratulate himself because he had shown acceptance toward a gay couple in his church. This may be an adequate expression of affirming love, accommodating this couple into his life, but it falls short of just love which would question the very terms upon which some people get to do the accepting and others must passively wait to be accepted — often having the acceptability of their lives and loves voted upon by those in the dominant majority. These are questions of social privilege and hierarchy that are central to considerations of justice.

But what exactly does an attitude of just love obligate us to do through our practices of ministry? The intentional and reflective asking of these questions within the context of a faith community should lead neither to assimilation of difference into the norm or simple accommodation of difference into the present structures (what I referred to in the Introduction as boundary maintenance). Rather, exploring these questions with an attitude of just love should lead to varied adaptive practices of ministry whereby our practices themselves shift, change, and evolve in relation to what we learn about their effects on the lives of those who are pushed to the margins of our communities.

Adaptive ministry will always seek to learn from those who embody some difference from the dominant norm within our communities. Adaptive ministry asks how the mirror held up to us in the life of the other exposes our own limited views of God, faith, ministry, etc. To be sure, adaptive ministry does not preclude the possibility of accommodating queer people into the present structures of church and community. However, just love requires that accommodation not take place without a sufficient questioning and critique of the current structures that have served to exclude and marginalize those who are now being gradually included. Sometimes the institutions, structures, and practices themselves are too closely tied to injustice and thus must be set aside or, in other cases, adapted to fit experiences and perspectives that differ from those for whom these institutions were designed.

For example, when we consider questions of marriage, we can simply plug same-sex couples into the mold set by heterosexual couples, accommodating queer lives into the institution of marriage. Or, from a just love, adaptational perspective, we might allow the unjust exclusion of queer people from this institution to give us pause, leading us to question what other forms of injustice might be perpetuated by our normative marital practices. Asking: Why do we distribute certain rights and benefits of a legal contract based solely upon a gendered and sexualized relationship?[25] How does the residue of patriarchy still linger in our modern conceptions of marriage?[26] How does our cultural and religious obsession with the question of marriage unnecessarily limit our views of relationship and family?[27]

The step that just love obligates us to take is simply this: We must continually step back from the questions of accommodation to ask the larger question, "What religious views and ministerial practices helped to cultivate the circumstances of injustice and marginalization in the first place?" It is in vigorously pursuing this inquiry that we are able to infuse our practices of love for marginalized individuals with the pursuit of justice that enhances the lives of all.

Continually Revisiting our Practices of Love

I once gave a public address on the complexities of love in relation to queer lives that contained many of the perspectives developed in this chapter. After my talk, another speaker took to the podium. If I could reduce this speaker's message to a sentence or two, it went something like this: "All of this sounds too complicated. All churches need to do is simply love gay people, and we'd all be a lot better off." Once I overcame the disappointment that my message had been so blatantly thwarted by the simplistic appeal of the "all-you-need-is-love" panacea, I came away from that experience with the realization that the one lesson we are all in need of learning is that love is not a straightforward cure for all that ails us. The intersections of queer lives and Christian practices of love demonstrate the complexity of what we often talk about with such commonsensical simplicity. Love for queer people does not mean the same thing to everyone who purports to practice it, nor is it always experienced as truly loving by those expected to receive it.

One lesson churches might learn from a closer look at normalizing love and assimilationist practices of ministry is the potential for dangerous consequences when religious, psychological, and legal discourses converge when addressing questions of human difference. Each of these discourses — religious, psychological, legal — represents a powerful way of naming reality — that is, describing what is real and true about our human experience. As we can see in both the historic instance of drapetomania and in more modern examples of homosexuality viewed as sin, sickness, and a danger to society, these powerful discourses can be easily used in ways that oppress and marginalize those who differ from the dominant group. We must take from this lesson a need for continued theological exploration of the ways we name what is real and true about our own lives and the lives of those who differ from us. Our exploration must give close attention to the voices and experience of the marginalized on their own terms, resisting the temptation to name reality for those who differ from us.

A second lesson we may learn from a stance of affirming love and accommodating practices of ministry is that the notion of love for queer people may, at times, serve only to make the present structures of church and society more accommodating to queer lives without calling the taken-for-granted nature of the status quo into question. We must continually be led to ask: "How did these institutions and structures come to exclude queer people in the first place?" And, "What other groups of people are being marginalized by these same institutions?"

The third, and perhaps most important, lesson we may learn from a stance of just love and adaptive practices of ministry for queer people is the need for an ever-greater fusion of love and justice that continues to ask difficult, critical questions about our religious communities, ministries, and practices of faith. These questions must be explored with an eye toward those who are marginalized by the current status quo, attempting to learn from their lives and experience. When we make this commitment, we not only endeavor to extend love to individuals who find themselves pushed to the margins of our churches and communities, but we commit ourselves to cultivating a better, more just pathway toward an ever-expanding circle of voices, moving us closer and closer to the practice of just love.

Love seems so simple, but it's often the simple, seemingly straightforward, commonsense elements of our faith that are in need of greatest critical probing. It is too easy to take for granted that we know what we mean when we say we love queer people, all the while missing the ways our love is wreaking havoc on queer lives or simply falling short of a more just expression of love. This type of self-critique can be difficult, but the stakes are high for churches endeavoring to practice Christian love for queer people. The stakes are also high for queer persons in our midst whose lives are often quite literally at stake. Now is the time for all of us to raise the stakes within our own churches to question our practices of ministry that operate under the guise of love for the other.

Notes

[1]Kelly Brown Douglas, *Sexuality and the Black Church: A Womanist Perspective* (Maryknoll, NY: Orbis, 1999), 5.

[2]These three questions are similar in their structure to the "Visional/ Metaphorical," "Obligation," and "Rules/Roles" stages of practical moral reasoning found in the work of Don Browning. In the framework represented here, Browning's "Tendencies/Needs" and "Social and Natural Environment" can be seen as folded into the first question. Though I am not following Browning's framework in any strict fashion, his thought influences the structure of these question in consideration of practices of love that emerge from churches' practical moral reasoning about sexuality. For more, see, Don S. Browning, *Religious Ethics and Pastoral Care* (Minneapolis: Fortress, 1983) and *A Fundamental Practical Theology: Descriptive and Strategic Proposals* (Minneapolis: Fortress, 1991).

[3]For a thorough exploration of the theological concept of "sin" from a queer theological perspective, see Patrick S. Cheng, *From Sin to Amazing Grace: Discovering the Queer Christ* (New York: Seabury Books, 2012).

[4]Since our focus here is to understand how "love" is practiced from varied perspectives and what we might learn from those practices, I have left the detailed biblical and theological arguments for each view out of the discussion. For readers interested in accessing a text that addresses these questions in detail from a diversity of perspectives, see Choon-Leong Seow, ed., *Homosexuality and Christian Community* (Louisville: Westminster John Knox, 1996).

[5]For a thorough exploration of the overlapping discourses of religion and science among Christian churches and denominations in the U.S. since the 1940s, see Mark

D. Jordan, *Recruiting Young Love: How Christians Talk About Homosexuality* (Chicago: University of Chicago Press, 2011).

[6]For a thorough exploration of the intertwining of religious and legal discourses, see Janet Jakobsen and Ann Pellegrini, *Love the Sin: Sexual Regulation and the Limits of Religious Tolerance* (New York: New York University Press, 2003).

[7]George Chauncey, *Why Marriage? The History Shaping Today's Debate Over Gay Equality* (New York: Basic Books, 2004), 11.

[8]Thomas Szasz, "The Sane Slave: An Historical Note on the Use of Medical Diagnosis as Justificatory Rhetoric," *American Journal of Psychotherapy* 25(2) (1971): 228-239, cited in Barry D. Adam, *The Survival of Domination: Inferiorization and Everyday Life* (New York: Elsevier, 1978), 35.

[9]This "biblical" justification of slavery is well illustrated in a sermon preached by The Reverend E. W. Warren at the First Baptist Church of Macon, Georgia, on January 27, 1861, titled "Scriptural Vindication of Slavery," which was printed in the Macon newspaper, *Daily Telegraph*, the following month (Feb. 7, 1861). In this sermon, Warren meticulously makes a "biblical" argument for the view that slavery is designed, ordained, and upheld as an institution by God.

[10]It is noteworthy that the first "ex-gay" group in the U.S., founded in 1973, was named "Love in Action." Its founding figure, Frank Worthen, spread the message that "a truly loving Christian community can help men exchange their homosexual identities for something better." Jordan, *Recruiting Young Love*, 151.

[11]"About Love Won Out," Exodus International, accessed February 7, 2013, http://exodusinternational.org/love-won-out/about-love-won-out/.

[12]"Help for People with Same-Sex Attractions," Exodus International, accessed February 7, 2013, http://exodusinternational.org/find-help/help-for-people-with-ssa/.

[13]For example, the practice of "reparative" or "conversion therapy" is congruent with the Code of Ethics upheld by the American Association of Christian Counselors. See section 1-126, which reads, "Christian counselors refuse to condone or advocate for the pursuit of or active involvement in homosexual, transgendered, and cross-dressing behavior, and in the adoption gay & lesbian & transgendered lifestyles by clients… Christian counselors differ, on biblical, ethical, and legal grounds, with groups who abhor and condemn reparative therapy, willingly offering it to those who come into counseling with a genuine desire to be set free of homosexual attractions and leave homosexual

behavior and lifestyles behind. Either goal of heterosexual relations and marriage or life-
long sexual celibacy is legitimate and a function of client choice in reparative therapy."
AACE Law and Ethics Committee, "AACC Code of Ethics" (2004), accessible for down-
load at http://www.aacc.net/about-us/code-of-ethics/.

[14]Once again, as the *practices of love* that flow from these theological understandings are the central focus of this chapter, the biblical and theological considerations
that lead churches to this perspective will not be addressed with any depth. For a helpful
example of the biblical and theological work that leads to the practice of "affirming love,"
see, Walter Wink, ed., *Homosexuality and Christian Faith: Questions of Conscience for the
Churches* (Minneapolis: Augsburg Fortress, 1999).

[15]Sigmund Freud, *Die Zeit*, October 27, 1903.

[16]For an overview of these statements, see "Reparative Therapy: Statements by
Professional Associations and Their Leaders," Religious Tolerance.org, accessed February
22, 2012, http://www.religioustolerance.org/hom_expr.htm (accessed February 22,
2012).

[17]"Open & Affirming Team," GLAD Alliance, accessed February 7, 2013,
http://www.gladalliance.org/open-affirming.

[18]"Open and Affirming in the UCC," United Church of Christ, accessed
February 7, 2013, http://www.ucc.org/lgbt/ona.html.

[19]Association of Welcoming and Affirming Baptists, accessed February 7,
2013, http://www.awab.org.

[20]For churches wishing to engage in conversation on the subject of same-sex
marriage from a progressive Christian perspective, see Gene Robinson, *God Believes in
Love: Straight Talk About Gay Marriage* (New York: Knopf, 2012).

[21]"Just Love" is the title of Margaret Farley's landmark text, *Just Love: A
Framework for Christian Sexual Ethics* (New York: Continuum, 2008). She defines this
term, stating, "A love is right and good insofar as it aims to affirm truthfully the concrete
reality of the beloved" (200). While the vision for "just love" that I develop in this section
is not entirely based on Farley's perspective, her title is eminently helpful in capturing the
fusion of love and justice that I aim toward here. Readers should note that Farley's text is
an astute, helpful and approachable resource for congregations wishing to explore questions of sexual ethics within a Christian theological tradition. Another appropriate term

for this type of love might be "radical love," which is the title of a recent text by Patrick S. Cheng, *Radical Love: An Introduction to Queer Theology* (New York: Seabury, 2011).

[22]Iris Marion Young, *Justice and the Politics of Difference* (Princeton, NJ: Princeton University Press, 1990), 16, 38.

[23]These encapsultate Young's definition of "domination" and "oppression." See Young, *Justice and the Politics of Difference*, 38.

[24]This question is shaped around Iris Marion Young's definition of "oppressions" which, she argues, is experience by structural, institutional, or systemic constraints that cause the inhibition of ability to develop and exercise one's capacities and express needs, thoughts, feelings, and perspectives on life in contexts where others can listen. See Young, *Justice and the Politics of Difference*, 38.

[25]For readers interested in exploring this question further, see Janet R. Jakobsen, "Queer Relations: A Reading of Martha Nussbaum on Same-Sex Marriage," *Columbia Journal of Gender and Law* 19(1) (2010): 133-177.

[26]For readers interested in exploring this question further, see Gerda Lerner, *The Creation of Patriarchy* (New York: Oxford University Press, 1986).

[27]This question can also be pursued further with the assistance of Jakobsen, "Queer Relations."

Chapter Five

Lessons on Violence

Not all lessons are positive. Some lessons, rather than pointing to our unrealized potential, must point out our most glaring flaws. These lessons are some of the most difficult to learn. One lesson that churches must learn at the intersection of Christian tradition and queer lives is a lesson on the violent potential of religion.

The idea that religion causes violence is a popular notion[1] with seemingly ample support in historical precedent: the brutality of the Crusades, the execution of heretics throughout Christian history, the witch trials, the history of violence between Catholics and Protestants in Northern Ireland, and myriad persecutions by Christians of religious and ethnic Others in every era. While I am not convinced that religion causes violence in any simple cause-and-effect way,[2] it is important to consider particular styles of thought — many of which appear with regularity in religious communities — that may cultivate a social sphere ripe for violence against those who are different in some way or another. In other words, we must take account of the ways our religious beliefs and practices support violence against queer people as a group embodying some difference from the dominant norm. The intersections of Christian tradition and the lives of queer people hold great potential for illuminating these dangerous patterns of violence emerging from our religious practice if we are willing to ask,

What can churches learn from queer experiences about religious con-
tributions to violence against different Others and what can be done to reduce
this violence?

Learning lessons from a bloody, gruesome reality like anti-
LGBTQ violence is a difficult prospect. Violence against innocent victims
should prompt us to act in their defense, not sit around thinking about
what we might learn from their experience. While action is the correct
response, unreflective action runs the risk of never fully addressing the
problem in its complexity. As South African Methodist minister, Trevor
Hudson, says, "Disorganized good is no match for organized evil."[3] The
actions we take in order to reduce violence against queer people must be
shaped by an inquiry into the contours of this violence so that we may
better understand the ways we all contribute, even unknowingly, to the
undue suffering of queer people.

As the question above implies, what we stand to learn from
this difficult lesson may transcend the relationship between Christian
tradition and queer lives. The lessons learned from religiously-fueled
anti-LGBTQ violence can help us to consider the relationship between
our theological beliefs and the actions these beliefs inspire in relation to
many others — the marginal, the different, the Other — with whom
we share a church, a community, a country, and a world. The lessons we
learn may, in short, help us to cultivate a less violent Christianity in relation to those we view as different.

Physical Violence: The Visible Wounds

While the meaning of "violence" may seem obvious, there are
many types of violence and it can be unhelpful to approach them as if
they are all the same. These various types have different and often complex causes, varied motives, and a wide range of different effects upon
those targeted.

There are interpersonal acts of violence in which perpetrators have the practical motive of material gain (robbery, for example). One person or group violently attacks another in order to steal their possessions. In this case, the violent act is only a means to an end. Other acts of interpersonal violence occur unplanned in the heat of the moment, motivated by anger following arguments, misunderstandings, and accidents. Bar fights, an argument among strangers that comes to blows, fist fights at sporting events — these interpersonal acts of violence serve no particular end aside from enacting the anger arising in the moment between two parties.

There are also institutional forms of violence through which entities — governments, for example — use violence for socially-sanctioned purposes, such as a military at war, police exerting force to subdue a perpetrator or control a crowd, and even state executions. The institution of government carries out its purposes for protection, retaliation, maintaining social order, etc., through acts of violence that are presumably performed on behalf of the collective of people represented by the entity or government. Individuals and collectives are employed to undertake institutional forms of violence, but they are acts of violence for specific social purposes.

But violence against queer people falls into a different category. It is a violence that cannot be explained by opportunistic gain or heat-of-the-moment interpersonal rage. Neither is it typically undertaken in a direct fashion by institutions.[4] Instead, violence against queer people can be described as an instrumental form of violence. It is instrumental in that it serves a function that extends far beyond the singular violent act against the individual victim. It is instrumental in the delivery of a precise message, motivated by ideological beliefs about the target of violence — in this case, queer people.[5] The violent act becomes the instrument by which these anti-queer beliefs are made visible. Specifically, violent acts against queer people undergird and carry forth the prevalent messages emanating from corridors of church and society that name queer people as objects of disgust, evidence of disorder, embodiments of sin, and presumed threats to a social order.

Iris Marion Young describes this type of violence as taking place when members of some groups are made subject to "random, unprovoked attacks on their persons or property, which have no motive but to damage, humiliate, or destroy the person," as well as "less severe incidents of harassment, intimidation, or ridicule simply for the purpose of degrading, humiliating, or stigmatizing group members."[6] While this type of violence often looks like simple interpersonal violence, it does not have as its aim personal material gain, nor does it typically arise in instances of interpersonal conflict due to an argument, an accident, or a misunderstanding. In these cases, violence is used as an instrument to reinforce an ideology of superiority through the publicly-violent degradation of minority group members.

Instances of instrumental violence are often fueled by widespread fear or hatred of groups such as women, racial minorities, religious minorities, gay, lesbian, bisexual, and transgender persons, and other groups targeted because of a perceived difference from the dominant majority. This violence is an instrument of group hatred and serves the instrumental purpose of physically enforcing the belief systems that make the targeted group an object of hatred. So in order to understand concerns of instrumental violence, we must look beyond the physical wounds of its victims to ask: Why was this person, specifically, targeted for attack? What beliefs about the victim's sexual orientation or gender identity caused this person to make sense as a viable target of violence? How is this violence an instrument of a more widespread hatred of queer people?

Hate crime violence is one particular type of instrumental violence that has become vitally important in considering the wellbeing of queer people in our society. Even since the signing of the 2009 Matthew Shepard and James Byrd, Jr. Hate Crimes Prevention Act into federal law, the violent attack and murder of lesbian, gay, bisexual, and transgender persons — as well as many who are simply presumed to be LGBT

— continues to cast an ominous pall over U.S. society. The National Coalition of Anti-Violence Programs reports that in 2011, there was an overall decrease of 16 percent in reports of hate violence against lesbian, gay, bisexual, transgender, queer, and HIV-affected persons. While this news seems consoling, their 2011 report also revealed the highest number of hate-motivated murders ever recorded by this organization, with people under the age of 30 most likely to be targeted.[7] Theologian Stephen V. Sprinkle sees these statistics pointing to "an epidemic of bias-driven hate murders perpetrated against the last great group in America it is still politically correct to dehumanize and harm."[8]

Many local police departments simply chalk these murders up to risky behavior on behalf of the victim, most do not garner the attention of the media, and the majority are ignored by communities not wishing to acknowledge the murder of their queer citizens (perhaps even more unwilling to acknowledge the lives of queer citizens). Queer people, too, often turn away from the spectacle of hate crime murders, attempting to preserve the illusion that perhaps the world isn't as brutal toward queer people as it sometimes appears. Still, some efforts are being made to honor the memory of these queer lives lost to hate crime murder. Some of these hate crime murder victims are remembered each year at the annual Transgender Day of Remembrance services held in cities across the country — many of which are hosted by local congregations. Many of these lost lives are memorialized in writing through the work of Stephen Sprinkle, who endeavors to help queer people do the difficult but important work of remembering our dead.[9]

Ignoring the gruesome reality of LGBTQ hate crime murder may temporarily shield us from the discomforting reality. But forgetting our queer dead is too easy. Congregations may even assuage their collective consciences through acts of remembrance, without taking the further step of examining the ways churches are complicit in cultivating a social space in which instrumental violence against queer people is not only possible, but probable. If we are willing to unflinching inquire into the lessons held for churches in the violent intersections of queer lives and religious traditions, we stand to learn a great deal that may help us in mounting a resistance to the oppressive force of instrumental violence.

The first important lesson we must learn about instrumental acts of hate crime violence is this: it's not just the "victim" that is victimized. All queer people are indirect targets of an act of violence that directly targets any one queer person simply because they are a part of a minority LGBTQ population. While a majority of queer people may avoid ever becoming the direct victim of a violent, bias-motivated crime, none will be able to avoid the terrorizing knowledge that is visited upon queer people with each reminder that this is a world in which people are maimed and killed because of their sexual orientation or gender identity. Iris Marion Young sums up the oppressive force of this terrorizing knowledge in this way:

> The oppression of violence consists not only in direct victimization, but in the daily knowledge shared by all members of oppressed groups that they are liable to violation, solely on account of their group identity. Just living under such a threat of attack on oneself or family or friends deprives the oppressed of freedom and dignity, and needlessly expends their energy.[10]

Queer people cannot afford to ignore the reality of violence against LGBTQ lives. Even when the potential for violence is not held within our conscious awareness, there is an embodied awareness that always maintains vigilance. This is not the hyper vigilance of paranoia; it is a necessary awareness for survival. It is an awareness that automatically scans the safety of a room, a street, a church, a town, asking: "Is this place safe for a queer person?" One intimate touch of a same-sex partner in the wrong locale holds the potential to draw taunts, jeers, or physical attack. The revelation — intentional or unintentional — of one's sexual orientation or gender identity may be the flint that sparks the fires of violence.

Queer spaces and gay ghettos — bars, neighbors, and gathering places — have often served as havens where the psychological vigilance can be lowered. But, at times, even these presumably safe spaces become the sites of unimaginable horror — infiltrated by those who wish to do us harm.

Thus, instrumental violence against queer people serves to curtail the freedom of queer people, maintaining a social sphere in which presenting oneself as anything other than heterosexual and gender-conforming is intermittently punishable by verbal assault or physical violence. The indignity of instrumental violence rests in its potential to ensure that queer people must, at certain times and in particular places, hide important information about their sense of self and their closest relationships — an indignity not known to straight people. The needless expenditure of energy caused by instrumental violence serves to keep queer minds always on guard, occupied with the knowledge that becoming the target of violent assault is never entirely out of the question.[11]

While hate crime violence against queer people may regularly escape our attention, the reality of anti-LGBTQ school bullying has been such a pervasive topic of public discussion in recent years that it is hard for anyone to ignore. The bullying of queer kids by their peers is another form of instrumental violence that is undergirded by a religious and cultural portrayal of queer lives as deserving of derision. While the physical damage of bullying may be less extensive than in cases of hate crime violence, the mechanisms that power the bullying of queer teens mirror the operations of instrumental violence and serve similar oppressive ends against the freedom and dignity of queer youth. While much of the bullying that takes place against queer young people has a physical component, some of the most persistent, cutting, and psychologically deteriorating forms of bullying are delivered in verbal form.

Microaggressions: The Subtle Violence of Everyday Speech

It is the violence that we don't notice that often wreaks the most havoc in the lives of queer people. The violence that never draws blood, that leaves no bruises, that never scars the body's exterior, but leaves its insidious marks upon the soul — this is the violence about which churches have the most to learn.

The childhood adage, "Sticks and stones may break my bones, but words can never hurt me," may be one of the most dangerous lies we tell our children. A lesson meant to help them toughen up in the face of childhood taunts also inadvertently communicates the message that words hold no real power — that they can't really deliver the damage of physical blows. But this is simply not true.

Aside from outright hate speech, in which the message and its intent to harm the recipient is made perfectly clear, the majority of damaging speech is not intentionally hateful. Nevertheless, in its subtlety, the message of queer disorder, disease, sinfulness, and social disdain are communicated in speech that often passes by the conscious awareness of the speaker. Like instrumental physical violence, this subtly aggressive speech carries forth ideological and theological messages that denigrate queer lives. These speech acts have come to be known as "microaggressions." Don't let the newness of the term scare you. The meaning is simple and we all encounter microaggressions on a daily basis.

Derald Wing Sue, professor of psychology at Columbia University, defines microaggressions as "brief, everyday exchanges that send denigrating messages to certain individuals because of their group membership."[12] Sue explains, "These exchanges are so pervasive and automatic in daily conversations and interactions that they are often dismissed and glossed over as being innocent and innocuous."[13] Thus, they are micro in that they are often spoken without the speaker's awareness that they are communicating an aggressive message about members of the targeted group. Nevertheless, they are aggressive in *the subtle denigrating message* they communicate about the group in question.

Sue, the leading expert in microaggression research, defines three distinct types of microaggressions:

1. **Microinsults**: Microinsults are so common that we've all spoken them without even being aware that we are doing so. Sue explains them this way:

> Microinsults are characterized by interpersonal or environmental communications that convey stereotypes, rudeness, and insensitivity and that demean a persons' racial, gender, or sexual orientation, heritage, or identity. Microinsults represent subtle snubs, frequently outside the conscious awareness of the perpetrator, but they convey an oftentimes hidden insulting message to the recipient.[14]

One example can be seen in the way church folk regularly speak of "gay people" and "Christians" as categories of persons that are mutually exclusive. The subtle, demeaning message communicates insensitivity to the reality that many queer persons *are* Christians and the two groups are not mutually exclusive. Thus, the all-too-common ways that sermons, debates, and everyday speech present queer people as a category in contradistinction to Christian people subtly communicates a stereotype of queer persons as anti-Christian, which comes through to queer ears no matter the overt message that is intended. The message is not necessarily intended to be directly hostile or aggressive. The speaker may not even be aware that the communication is performing in this insulting way. Nevertheless, it comes through as an insulting communication to those who are both Christian and queer.

2. **Microinvalidations**: Rather than insult a recipient based upon their sexuality or gender identity, microinvalidations render one's particular experience as a lesbian, gay, bisexual, transgender, or queer person invalid. It is important to keep in mind that, just like microinsults, microinvalidations are communicating an aggressive message that

is not necessarily intentional and is perhaps even outside of the awareness of the speaker. Sue describes them, saying,

> Microinvalidations are characterized by communications or environmental cues that exclude, negate, or nullify the psychological thoughts, feelings, or experiential realities of certain groups, such as people of color, women and LGBTs . . . they directly and insidiously deny the racial, gender, or sexual-orientation reality of these groups.[15]

Take, for example, a sermon about marriage delivered in a church in which there are queer people and perhaps even same-sex couples in the congregation. If the sermon consistently refers to "husband and wife," it subtly invalidates the reality that some intimate partnerships are between two men or two women. Additionally, even a sermon on marriage in a congregational context attempting to welcome lesbian and gay persons may become subtly invalidating to same-sex couples if the congregation is located in a state in which marriage is legally unavailable or in a congregation that doesn't yet perform marriage ceremonies for same-sex couples. In this case, to avoid the microinvalidation of queer people in the congregation, a sermon might be crafted around the theological notion of covenanted relationships rather than marriage, and the social inequality upheld in states without same-sex marriage may be openly recognized and prophetically challenged in the sermon.

Another example of a microinvalidation that is communicated by environmental cues, rather than verbally, involves something many of us take for granted: restrooms. Nearly all restrooms in every church, business, and public space come in two forms labeled "Men" and "Women." For many of us, there is no hesitation about which restroom to enter. For a transgender person, however, the dually-identified bathrooms pose a dilemma. When one's physiology doesn't accord with one's psychological and spiritual sense of gender, choosing which bathroom to use becomes more complex. If one is at some point in the process of transition through surgical or hormonal procedure, from male physiology to female or female to male, the dichotomous choice between the "Male" and "Female" restrooms can't be made so easily. When a building doesn't offer a gender-neutral restroom, the physical space itself communicates a microinvalidating message. The subtle communication is simple, but profoundly painful: We didn't anticipate your existence, thus there is no place for you here.

3. **Microassaults**: Microassaults, unlike microinsults and microinvalidations, are far less subtle and can even be intentional forms of aggressive speech against targeted people. Nevertheless, they are micro in the sense that they are often not delivered as an outright slight against a specific target. Sue describes them this way:

> Microassaults are conscious, deliberate, and either subtle or explicit racial, gender, or sexual-orientation biased attitudes, beliefs, or behaviors that are communicated to marginalized groups through environmental cues, verbalizations, or behaviors . . . The intent of these messages is to threaten, intimidate, and make the individuals or groups feel unwanted and unsafe because they are inferior, subhuman, and lesser beings that do not belong on the same levels as others in this society.[16]

Sue believes that microassaults may be the most common form of microaggression experienced by LGBT persons.[17] An example might be an impassioned diatribe against queer persons made by a pastor or Sunday School teacher that communicates overtly denigrating messages about queer lives. Churches that refuse the embrace of church membership or the rite of baptism to queer people may also communicate a microassaulting message both to those within the congregation and to those on the outside looking in — a message that says, "You are inferior, subhuman, lesser beings." Microassaults are delivered most easily when the speaker is in the presence of those believed to agree with the assessment of queer people being expressed, relying on the timidity and refusal of others to challenge the speaker.[18]

As careful as we might be with our speech, we all enact microagressions in ways we never realize. To be clear, what is at stake in the discussion of microaggressions against queer people is not the tepid matter of being politically correct. Microaggressions operate as a form of violence, serving the same instrumental functions as physical violence — curtailing the freedom of queer people to openly live their lives and express their loves, subtly degrading queer lives through insult and invalidation, and unnecessarily occupying their psychological and emotional energy. What is at stake is the cultivation of a more just social and ecclesial space.

Sue describes this depletion of psychological energy as one of the most damaging effects of microaggressions. Because they are micro — subtle and often fuzzy in their true intention and meaning — a person targeted by a microaggression cannot ever be certain of the speaker's motive or the real meaning behind the message. This "attributional ambiguity," as Sue calls it, means that those targeted by microaggressions can never be sure how to respond. Confronting the speaker may be met with a simple denial of the presumably unintended and misunderstood message and may even cause more overt ire to be heaped upon the now "overly sensitive" queer person. Thus, Sue states that the most frequent response to a microaggression is to do nothing.[19]

While those targeted by the instrumental violence of physical assault and the subtle psychological tyranny of microaggressions may have little recourse in the moment, these forms of violence often have horrifying effects in the lives of queer people — especially our queer youth.

Queer Suicide: When Violence Gets Inside Us

In September of 2010, I sat in front of my computer screen in disbelief. It had been a difficult few weeks of sadness as I witnessed story after story in the news of LGBTQ teenagers killing themselves. The media revealed that for most of these queer kids, bullying was a daily reality — verbally and physically attacked by their peers, often receiving very little help from the adults in their schools. And the list that month was long: Billy Lucas, 15 years old; Seth Walsh, 13; Tyler Clementi, 18; Harrison Chase Brown, 15; Asher Brown, 13; Caleb Nolt, 14; Raymond Chase, 19. By early October, as I sat in front of my computer once again reading the breaking news of another queer teen taking his own life, my sadness turned to anger. These were not depressed teens, succumbing to unbearable psychological pain. These were all young victims of a comprehensive culture of violence brought to bear upon queer lives.

On the surface, suicide may seem unrelated to a discussion of violence against queer people. Aside from the possible connection to bullying, what does a queer person's suicide have to do with the larger reality of violence against queer people? While suicide represents an intensely personal decision to end one's own life, it is also the most potent illustration of the ability of anti-queer instrumental violence to penetrate beneath the skin — to get inside us. It is evidence of violence against the soul of queer people.

Violence against the queer soul is a particularly insidious type of violence, the impact of which cannot be assessed by examining bruises. It amounts to more than a simple violent act against a queer person by a homophobic attacker. Violence against queer people in any form is an ideologically aggravated, theologically intensified violence. It is an act of violence legitimated by an inseparable social and theological discourse about queer people that is already embedded in the lives of both attacker and victim. With this theological intensification, violence against queer people — whether by physical blow or the microaggressive operations of verbal and environmental cues — penetrates beneath the skin, communicating something about how the queer self is seen by the perpetrator and society as a whole, attempting to induce the same queer-denigrating view into the psyche of the queer person.

Even while violent perpetrators and their enablers must be held accountable for the damage done by a bully's blows, queer suicide is not the simple, direct result of bullying. There is instead a sinister alchemy that takes place by which the physical attack and verbal harassment of peers is transformed, becoming the tangible outworking of a much larger social and theological discourse denigrating queer lives. These are fists with footnotes. While the physical blows and verbal barbs are the method of delivery, the real message is in the citation of larger religious and social messages that denigrate queer people. These queer-denigrating messages mark the queer body as an appropriate target for acts of insult, hatred, and violence. They occupy queer minds with the unsettling knowledge that always and everywhere we are liable to become victims of violent attack just for bringing our queerness to light.

Insults like "fag," often combined with physical assault, become citations of social and religious portrayals of the queer self as sick, sinful, or an object of disgust and derision — images that swirl in social consciousness long before blows are brought to bear upon queer bodies. But these social-religious discourses not only make queer bodies eligible for attack. They also provide available material out of which queer people come to construct a sense of self. Often encountered very early in life, these messages become part of the lens through which queer people develop a sense of their own core identity — or soul. Even when consciously disavowing messages that "queer" means somehow being sick or sinful, these discourses nevertheless become a part of a queer social self.

Didier Eribon captures this reality in a hauntingly poignant paragraph in his book, *Insult and the Making of the Gay Self.* Eribon writes,

> [A] gay subjectivity is formed through a process of self-education, through a severe self-discipline that can never be relaxed, that must scrutinize every move, with the goal of appearing to be 'as normal as everyone else.'

The long-term effects of insult and hatred . . . write
themselves into the body; they act by way of your own
submission to the injunction that they carry, your own
consent to the order they enforce — that your personal-
ity and your desires must remain hidden, that the line
must be toed. They command you always to act 'as if.'
They necessitate a permanent effort to ensure that none
of your emotions, feelings, or desires are ever revealed.[20]

As Eribon reiterates, this is a violence that attacks the freedom,
erodes the dignity and unduly saps the energy of queer people leading
to physical, mental, and spiritual exhaustion and, in some instances,
suicide.[21]

Of course "queer" is not synonymous with "suicide," as it too
often seems. Not every queer person is on the brink of despair and self-
destruction. Not every queer person is bullied by their peers or rejected
by their parents. Not every queer person is vulnerable to depression or
has a suicide plan mapped out and at the ready. But queer suicide should
alarm us as it offers a poignant and disturbing reminder of the way in
which instrumental violence not only marks the body, but also gets inside
us to tear at the fabric of our soul.

And the Whole Church Says, "So What?"

So what? Even if churches see violence against queer people as a
deplorable problem, what is there for churches to learn from this? Many
congregations and religious groups already support the work of other
community organizations in addressing problems like anti-LGBTQ
school bullying. Still other churches and denominations have made
public professions of affirmation and solidarity with queer people who
face the realities of violence in our society. But, as I hope we are beginning to understand, treating the acts of violence without giving attention

to their religious undercurrents is only a partial and ultimately ineffective response to instrumental violence against queer lives.

It is certainly overly simplistic to say that religion causes violence against queer people. But it is both accurate and crucial for churches to confess the role that religious beliefs have held in fueling violence against queer lives. Our theologies have played a central role in cultivating a climate in which queer people regularly become the targets of violence. Some of the religious fuel for the notion that queer people are sick or sinful or a threat to society was explored in the previous chapter's lessons on love. Here, it becomes helpful to add to this material an understanding of a few particular religious styles of thought that contribute to violence against those who embody some form of difference — whether that be a racial, ethnic, religious, gender, or sexual identification that differs from the dominant norm.

The usual culprits are not solely to blame for violence against queer people. Though we might like to pin the responsibility on groups like Westboro Baptist Church, which made the phrase "God hates fags" famous through their raucous picketing at the funerals of fallen U.S. soldiers, we can't be so hasty in assigning blame. While the red-faced ranting of groups like Westboro is easily condemned and summarily dismissed by nearly every mainline or Evangelical congregation, we must also look carefully and critically at our own role in the perpetuation of anti-queer violence. There are two primary ways that churches often unknowingly lend credence to the theological currents that undergird this violence.

First, when we ask the question, "Why are queer people so often singled out for violent attack?" we must confront the dangers inherent in binary thinking. Binary thinking divides reality into black-and-white dualistic categories. Think of a few common examples that shape the way we categorize people: male/female, straight/gay, young/old, wealthy/poor. When binary, dualistic thinking comes to shape our theology it produces strong divisions like good/evil, holy/profane, heaven/earth, light/dark, etc. The simplistic, black-and-white lines that are drawn between conceptions of good and evil make it all-too-easy to apply these dualisms to our binary divisions between groups of people. When theologies leave no room for ambiguity, mystery and curiosity, it becomes very easy to identify an "us" (good, heterosexual) versus a "them" (evil, queer).

Pastoral theologian James Farris further explains the violent propensities contained in this style of thought, arguing that dualistic thought has become such a norm in theology and spirituality that what should be considered unities have been perceived as irreconcilable opposites. "More importantly," he argues," dualistic ways of viewing creation have allowed, and continue to allow, the denigration or negation of those not defined as useful, valuable, viable, and so forth by the dominant group or culture."[22] When the religious binary divisions between straight and queer join the host of social portrayals of queer people as diseased, disordered, and sinful, it is no wonder queer people come to seem appropriate targets for violent attack, as they are rendered not only passively useless and devoid of value, but actively aberrant and a danger to the rest of "us."

But the dangerous path into instrumental violence against queer people doesn't stop with binary thinking. The danger of instrumental violence exponentially increases when these binary categories (male/female, straight/gay) become theologically intensified through hierarchies of value and worth. Not only does one side of the binary division become validated as inherently more valuable as the other is deemed of lesser value, the value and worth of a particular group are also made to seem legitimate by the group's placement on a theological hierarchy. In this hierarchy, value and worth are not distributed equally; God is at the top, straight white men with capital come soon after and all those less valued by society (women, children, queer people, the poor, racial minorities, etc.) fall somewhere down below.[23] These binary divisions between groups and hierarchical arrangements that are often legitimated with "biblical" or "theological" rationales provide the structure of religious fuel for a host of social evils from slavery, to racial segregation, to genocides, to the subjugation of women, to instrumental violence against queer people.

In this light, it become clear that hate groups like Westboro are only the tip of a religious iceberg of instrumental violence and no faith group or congregation can rest in comfortable assurance that their own beliefs, teachings, and practices are free from complicity.[24] After all, it isn't always what we believe and teach about sexuality and gender identity, but how we think theologically about the meaning of human difference that is the root of the problem of instrumental violence. Churches that become concerned about instrumental violence against queer lives might begin addressing this concern by engaging in dialogue around a few important questions:

- How do our religious teachings about human difference get translated into action?

- How do our theologies come to be inscribed upon the souls of those in our congregations and communities, both in ways that are life giving and in ways that are violently debilitating?

- How can we take greater responsibility for our own theological teachings, as well as practice accountability with our friends, pastors, sister congregations, and denominations for the teachings they propagate about queer lives?

- How can we, as a congregation, take practical steps toward the reduction of violence against queer people in our community?

These are inquiries that can be discussed by any church or religious community, no matter their particular stance on questions of same-sex marriage, the welcome and affirmation of LGBTQ people, etc. If churches become appropriately disturbed by the violent intersections of queer lives and Christian tradition and are willing to ask more expansive questions than those to which we have grown accustomed, congregations may even forge new partnerships that transcend political divisions and theological differences in order to cultivate practical coalitions toward the reduction of instrumental violence against queer people.

The lessons we learn about violence at the intersection of queer lives and Christian tradition transcend their usefulness in addressing violence against queer people alone. These forms of violence (physical attack, microaggressions, and the violence that strikes the soul), as well as the theological styles of thought that fuel instrumental violence (binary divisions and hierarchical arrangements of value and worth) will continue to operate against different "Others" long after violence against queer people has diminished. Churches that learn to learn from queer lives about the terror of instrumental violence are well on their way to recognizing these patterns and practices of violence when they emerge against other groups targeted by instrumental violence. Out of a more complex understanding of the operations of instrumental violence, these churches may form the vanguard in shaping practices of care and justice toward those who exist at the margins of society.

Notes

[1] In recent years, there has been a plethora of texts expounding upon this notion. For example, see Mark Juergensmeyer, *Terror in the Mind of God: The Global Rise of Religious Violence*, 3rd ed. (Berkeley, CA: University of California Press, 2003).

[2] For a helpful treatment of the popular notion that "religion causes violence," see William T. Cavanaugh, *The Myth of Religious Violence: Secular Ideology and the Roots of Modern Conflict* (New York: Oxford, 2009).

[3] Trevor Hudson, plenary address given at the Cooperative Baptist Fellowship Leadership Institute, Fort Worth, Texas, June 20, 2012.

[4] There are notable exceptions to this in history. For example, in Nazi Germany, known gay people were interned in concentration camps. Likewise, in the mid-20th Century U.S., police brutality against LGBT people, lengthy incarceration, and unprovoked raids of gay bars were typical occurrences. This type of police brutality against

queer persons continues today in the U.S. and around the world and can be viewed as an overlap of institutional and instrumental violence.

⁵It must be noted that these "types" of violence are often overlapping. The overlap of instrumental violence with institutional violence can be seen particularly in cases when the law exacerbates the vulnerability of some groups, unduly exposing them to violence as in cases where hate crime protections are not extended to targeted groups. The institutional/instrumental combination can also be seen in times when the governmental structures become the servant of instrumental violence, as in a pre-civil rights era U.S. in which *political/legal force* was explicitly used to subjugate black persons to the *ideology* of White supremacy or in unprovoked police raids on known gay bars. The blend might also be seen in the well-documented racial bias inherent in the implementation of capital punishment and in myriad cases in which the ethnic, racial, cultural, or religious prejudices in dominant socio-political ideology fuels the aggression of international conflict and war. In yet other ways, interpersonal and instrumental violence overlaps in instances of domestic abuse and rape, in which a perpetrator's acts (interpersonal violence) may be motivated, legitimated, or overlooked due to ideological constructions (instrumental violence) of gender.

⁶Iris Marion Young, *Justice and the Politics of Difference* (Princeton, NJ: Princeton University Press, 1990), 61.

⁷The National Coalition of Anti-Violence Programs, *Hate Violence Against Lesbian, Gay, Bisexual, Transgender, Queer, and HIV-affected Communities in the United States in 2011* (New York: New York City Gay & Lesbian Anti-Violence Project, Inc., 2012), accessed January 25, 2013, http://www.avp.org/storage/documents/Reports/2012_NCAVP_2011_HV_Report.pdf.

⁸Stephen V. Sprinkle, "Until the Subject Changes: Reading & Telling Stories of Our Murdered LGBTQ Ancestors," in *Rightly Dividing the Word of Truth: A Resource for Congregations in Dialogue on Sexual Orientation and Gender Identity*, 2nd ed., ed. Cody J. Sanders (Charlotte, NC: Baptist Peace Fellowship of North America, 2013), 125.

⁹The lesson of remembrance is one to which theologian Stephen V. Sprinkle has dedicated a great deal of time and effort in recent years, producing a book, *Unfinished Lives: Reviving the Memories of LGBTQ Hate Crimes Victims* (Eugene, OR: Resource Publications, 2011), and maintaining a blog regularly updated with the stories of LGBTQ persons violently attacked and killed worldwide (www.unfinishedlivesblog.com).

[10]Young, *Justice and the Politics of Difference*, 62.

[11]For a scholarly social scientific treatment of this type of violence and the ways violence based upon the sexuality of a victim also interacts with the racial and gender identifications of those victims, see Gail Mason, *The Spectacle of Violence: Homophobia, Gender and Knowledge* (New York: Routledge, 2002). Mason also helpfully illuminates the theories of violence as an instrument that emerge from feminist theory and the scholarship of Michel Foucault.

[12]Derald Wing Sue, *Microaggressions in Everyday Life: Race, Gender, and Sexual Orientation* (Hoboken, NJ: John Wiley & Sons, 2010), xvi.

[13]Sue, *Microaggressions*, 25.

[14]Sue, *Microaggressions*, 31.

[15]Sue, *Microaggressions*, 37.

[16]Sue, *Microaggressions*, 28.

[17]Sue, *Microaggressions*, 108.

[18]Sue, *Microaggressions*, 30.

[19]Sue, *Microaggressions*, 54-55.

[20]Didier Eribon, *Insult and the Making of the Gay Self*, trans. Michael Lucey (Durham, NC: Duke University Press, 2004), 98-99.

[21]Through qualitative research interviews with young gay suicide attempters, Dorais found that rather than depression, his respondents instead showed signs of *exhaustion*. See Michel Dorais, *Dead Boys Can't Dance: Sexual Orientation, Masculinity, and Suicide*, with Simon L. Lajeunesse, trans. Pierre Tremblay (Montreal & Kingston: McGill-Queen's University Press, 2004), 81.

[22]James R. Farris, "The Ontology of Violence," in *Pastoral Theology's & Pastoral Psychology's Contributions to Helping Heal a Violent World*, ed. by G. Michael Cordner (Surakarta, Indonesia: The International Pastoral Care Network for Social Responsibility and DABARA Publishers, 1996), 120.

[23]Farris, "The Ontology of Violence," 119.

[24]Perhaps the most glaring example of the ways we all so often slide into dichotomous thinking about human lives — stripping others of their complexity — can be seen in the ways gay and lesbian identified persons regularly "explain away" the reality of *bisexual* people, saying "They're just on the fence," or "They just haven't made up their mind yet," or "They're just hanging onto their heterosexual privilege." Bisexual people

— those who experience physical and emotional attraction both to men and to women — do not fit neatly into dichotomous categories like straight/gay. It is also indicative of our attachment to binary categorizations of humanity that transgender persons are so often targeted for violence and become subject to exclusion, even within larger lesbian and gay circles. Once again, those who do not fit neatly into binary categories of male/ female trouble our easy, clear-cut methods of "making sense" of human embodiment.

Chapter Six

Lessons on Forgiveness

After a chapter on the insidious nature of violence against queer people, it is difficult to write about forgiveness. Forgiveness is not my first impulse in response to the history of anti-LGBTQ brutality in the United States. and the world over. Another difficulty in addressing forgiveness in relation to violence against LGBTQ people is the complexity of the problem and the deep, intractable damage this violence has done to queer lives. But in a book that invites churches to learn important lessons by inquiring compassionately and curiously into the lives of queer people, the real difficulty with lessons on forgiveness is that churches are the transgressors most in need of forgiveness.

As explored in the previous chapter, violence against queer people is an instrumental form of violence that serves to curtail the freedom of queer people, maintaining a social sphere in which presenting oneself as anything other than heterosexual and biologically gender conforming is intermittently punishable by verbal assault or physical violence. The specter of violence ensures that queer people must, at certain times and in particular places, hide important information about their sense of self and their closest relationships — an indignity not known in heterosexual relationships. Instrumental violence results in the needless expenditure of energy, keeping queer minds always on guard, occupied with the knowledge that becoming the target of violent assault is never entirely out of the question. It is carried forth by intermittent violent attack, but even more commonly in threatening verbalizations, the taunting and bullying of queer adolescents, and the everyday insults and invalidations that get "under the skin" of queer people, assailing the soul.

While churches are not directly responsible for each individual act of violence perpetrated against queer people, the culpability of communities of faith in cultivating an atmosphere in which acts of violence against LGBTQ people are thinkable is nearly undeniable. The persistence with which Christian churches have portrayed LGBTQ people as unnatural, dangers to society, predators of our children, and general objects of disgust and derision — emblematic of the "evil" which "good" Christians are to stand against — weaves a perverse web of violence within which we must live our lives. No one need lay a hand on a queer body in order for a queer person to be confronted with the knowledge that we live in a society in which LGBTQ people are always and everywhere at greater risk of attack solely because of an embodiment of difference in sexual orientation or gender identity.

For queer people coming to recognize the complexity of the violence perpetrated against us, fueled by the rhetoric of Christian theologizing and moralizing, we would do well to consider the question theologian John Swinton poses: "How can we faithfully hold onto the tensions among the command to forgive, the desire for revenge, and the need to ensure that justice and hope are available for both the victims and the perpetrators of evil?"[1] Since churches have played a prime role in the cultivation of an atmosphere of instrumental violence against queer lives, questions of forgiveness, revenge, justice, and hope shift the position of communities of faith from the oft-assumed teachers and brokers of forgiveness and justice to the position of perpetrators in need of contrite repentance.

This chapter is not intended to address the ways individual victims of violence might approach forgiveness or the place of forgiveness in the lives of those who have lost a loved one to hate crime violence. Instead of individual acts of forgiveness, this chapter asks what lessons churches and queer people stand to learn about the place of forgiveness in a collective sense, asking,

What can we all learn about the potential of forgiveness as a tool for peace and justice in addressing social conditions of injustice and violence?[2]

Mesach Krisetya writes, "It is not enough in this day and age that people hear the gospel of peace, they must see the gospel actually making peace. The genuine responsibility of religion to the society is that of prophetic witness."[3] But, as ethicist Karen Lebacqz is quick to remind us, Christianity has long served as an instrument in the reign of injustice, rather than a prophetic voice for the cultivation of peace. Lebacqz sees churches frequently serving as tools for the spread of terror, injustice, and repression.[4] We need not dig too deeply into Christian history to find examples of this spread of terror, injustice, and repression — whether enacted against women throughout history, racial minorities in the United States, the missionary zeal with which churches undergirded a history of worldwide colonial domination, or the ubiquitous religious persecution of non-Christians in every era and locale. But the particularities of our contemporary setting in the twenty-first century United States betray Christianity's particularly unrepentant spread of terror and violence against LGBTQ people.

While it seems telling that the remarkable gains queer people have made toward justice, inclusion, and equality in the Unites States have largely come without violent revolt — proving to be a very peaceable transformation in the realm of human rights — the violence enacted against queer people in this transformation of society has been quite severe. But rather than queer voices becoming strained by the incessant call upon churches to witness to the gospel of peace by turning from their wicked ways of violence and contritely seeking the forgiveness of queer people, we have the opportunity to take this prophetic mantle of peace upon ourselves. Queer people may become the prophetic witnesses to the gospel of peace that the majority of churches are currently unwilling to become in relation to LGBTQ justice.

Forgive Us Our Trespasses? The Deniability of Complex Wrongdoing

Many churches have made great strides toward the welcome and affirmation of LGBTQ people, exhibiting affirming love for queer lives and practicing accommodation of queer people into the structures of churches and denominations. Still others have taken further steps beyond welcome and affirmation toward a robust justice-seeking love for queer people, striving to change and reshape institutional and social structures into more just, equitable forms. But the reality remains that the vast majority of U.S. churches remain unconcerned at best and, at worst, virulently opposed to social and ecclesial equality and justice for LGBTQ people.

If history is any indication, many churches may never recognize their contributions to the cultivation of instrumental violence against queer lives. And when some of them eventually do, the realization will come far too late to produce an especially meaningful apology to those whose lives have been most profoundly affected by this violence.[5] Much like the damage caused by microaggressions (see previous chapter), the consequences of instrumental violence are largely invisible to churches and very easy to deny — the everyday subtle indignities, the shaping of behaviors in order to avoid public ridicule or violent attack that diminishes the freedom of life and expression of love, the needless expenditure of psychological energy in watchful vigilance, and the myriad ways inequality and injustice are embedded into the fabric of our social practices and institutions. When there is no literal blood on your hands, it's easy to say you play no part in practices of violence.

The potential for deniability of churches' complicity in the cultivation of instrumental violence against queer lives is great. Moreover, the damage perpetrated against queer lives through the complex workings of instrumental violence cannot be easily rectified or brought to justice through typical means. Even the flamboyant anti-gay hatred of groups like Westboro Baptist Church in Topeka, Kansas — the church that pickets the funerals of fallen U.S. soldiers with colorful signage reading "God Hates Fags" — cannot be easily remedied. Many in the United States believe — and the Supreme Court concurs — that the freedom of speech is a right worthy of protecting even if there are those who would regularly abuse it and gravely insult their fellow citizens in the process.

While we can prosecute hate crimes and legislate against discrimination, the harm perpetrated by many churches in the perpetuation of vocal hate or silent disdain for queer people is the sort that strikes at the invisibilities of the psyche and soul and rests beyond the reach of the legal system. And, while Westboro's flashy hatred of "fags" seems outlandish, it is but an aggravated and intensified form of the anti-LGBTQ discourses that circulate in many sectors of religious and civic life.

The likelihood is that a vast many churches and religious groups will never openly acknowledge their wrongdoing in relation to instrumental violence against queer people — at least not in the short-term. But this is not a case in which "forgive them, for they know not what they do" is an appropriate attitude. Even when it becomes clear the effect anti-queer religious teachings have upon the lives of LGBTQ people, even when they do know what they do, when groups like Westboro even mean to do it, still many have no intention of stopping. Above all, the vast majority may never seek forgiveness, even long after they have stopped producing the kind of public rhetoric that fuels widespread disdain for LGBTQ people and makes us targets of violence.

So what is the place of forgiveness in all of this? Open condemnation — while perhaps effective up to a point — seems only to stoke the embers of many churches' persecution-sensitivity, as many have come to believe that the increase of rights and protections for LGBTQ people places their own religious freedoms in jeopardy. Forgiveness almost seems nonsensical in the face of such grievous and unrepentant malice against queer people. But it is the surprising and even absurd place of forgiveness that makes it an especially effective response to instrumental violence. While many churches may never speak the words, "forgive us our trespasses," in relation to anti-queer violence, we should consider in what ways it is meaningful to imagine queer collectives saying publicly, "We forgive those churches that trespass against us." Most importantly, what lessons can we all learn from the possibilities of this queer forgiveness?

As We Forgive Those Who Trespass Against Us: Reimagining Forgiveness and Justice

When no one is breaking the law and no physical or financial harm is being perpetrated, we often have a difficult time discerning what justice has to do with the situation. When addressing cases like Westboro alongside the myriad cases of more mundane denigration of queer people through theological language and religious rhetoric, our conception of justice must transcend legal frameworks.

When it comes to justice, what is at stake in this case is the continued cultivation of a climate in which some among us (in this case, LGBTQ people) live amid soul-damaging, collectively denigrating discourses that are bolstered by the strong rhetorical capacity of religious language and symbol. This climate leaves many to live with the psychic terror of knowing that the discourse is, at times, enacted physically through violent attack and at all times holds potential to take up residence in our deepest sense of self or soul.

So while the legal system can be used to bring about a more equitable society in which rights, social privileges, and protections are extended to those targeted by discrimination and physical violence, it will fail to address many of the most damaging effects of instrumental violence — an issue of justice that transcends legality. Thus, in addressing the complexities of violence that cannot often be reached by legal protections, or legislation that provides for the equal distribution of rights and protections, or a balancing of payments between victim and perpetrator, forgiveness holds the potential to become a more subversive tool for peace and justice.

The difficulty comes in the way our thinking about forgiveness is often so dependent upon a model of economics and the supposed "balancing of the scales" we've become accustomed to in the legal system. As John Caputo argues, our typical "economies of forgiveness" rely upon a balance of payments — the offender must confess and feel contrite, make some effort at restitution, and commit to ceasing the wrongdoing.[6] Only then does the offended party extend forgiveness. In the case of the majority of churches complicit in the cultivation of instrumental violence against queer people, this economy of forgiveness is virtually impossible, as there is often no recognition of wrong, much less feelings of contrition or efforts at restitution.

In offering a different conception of forgiveness — one that will serve as an operative definition for this consideration of forgiveness as a subversive tool for peace and justice in relation to anti-LGBTQ violence — Caputo states:

> If forgiveness is to be anything more than economics, if it is to be a gift, then it must be an unconditional expenditure. Yet unconditional forgiveness looks like madness, implying that one could only forgive someone who is still offending, who does not deserve it, who has not earned it, but upon whom it is bestowed 'graciously' — or should we say, gratuitously. We would forgive those who are guilty and unrepentant and who have no intention, now or in the future, of making restitution or of sinning no more.[7]

Instead of an economy of power — the power to hold others responsible for their wrongdoing, to enact the conditions of forgiveness and the power to either extend or withhold forgiveness — Caputo argues that forgiveness entails a giving up of the power that one has over the other.[8] Forgiveness is a weak force.

Rather than waiting for the offender to enact the conditions of forgiveness and thus, according to the economy model, warrant forgiveness, forgiveness as a weak force[9] is truly unconditional. It is not uncommon to hear churches speak of unconditional forgiveness — many queer people have been told that this is what awaits us when we turn from our queer, sinful ways. But what is typically meant by unconditional forgiveness is that the offender must first ask for forgiveness — repenting and turning from their wicked ways, intending to sin no more. Forgiveness as a weak force, however, extends forgiveness to those who are still offending (sinning) and who have little or no intention of stopping.[10]

Caputo goes on to challenge the popular notions within powerful economies of forgiveness that one is to "forgive the sinner but not the sin" — also a phrase familiar to queer ears. Instead, Caputo argues that in the moment of sinning, the sinner and the sin are one so that to forgive the sinner but not the sin is to only forgive up to a point. "It is to forgive that part of the sinner that did not sin in the past and will not sin in the future, but not that part of the sinner that has been sinning and so needs forgiveness."[11] Forgiveness as a weak force extends forgiveness in the midst of continued offense with no expectation that the offense will cease and certainly with no expectation that the offender will repent and enact any rigorous set of conditions to meet requirements for forgiveness.

But forgiveness that is offered to offenders in the midst of their wrongdoing, when they have no intention of stopping, and when accountability cannot be rendered through strong methods like the force of law, holds greater potential for our work toward justice than the typical economies of forgiveness. Its potential rests in the ability of forgiveness to subvert the perpetrators' denial of their wrongdoing by openly naming the wrong, not with the strength of continued condemnation, but through the weak force of forgiveness.[12] When accountability cannot be rendered for the violence perpetrated against the invisibilities of self and soul, unsolicited forgiveness holds the potential to subversively challenge acts of hate while calling the attention of both perpetrators and on-looking witnesses to the gravity of the wrongdoing and the necessity for a better way toward a more just future.

Forgiving offenders who will not repent draws attention to the reality that the offense is occurring in the first place, even when perpetrators will not own up to it but its effects are deeply felt by those targeted. Without the repentance of the offender and in the absence of any accountability, forgiveness becomes a subversive call to the offender and to all who witness the absurd enactment of forgiveness to recognize that a grave wrong is taking place. Without drawing upon force of power to hold offenders accountable or to punish wrongdoing, the weak force of forgiveness becomes an unconditional gift offered on behalf of collectives of queer people — all victims of instrumental violence — having the subversive effect of calling attention to the wrong being perpetrated by offenders whose capacity for denial is still great.

Even as queer people are the obvious targets of instrumental violence, fueled and legitimated by religious teaching and Christian rhetoric, churches, too, are damaged by their continued culpability. As political philosopher P. E. Digeser argues,

> One of the complexities is that wrongs diminish both victims and transgressors. The transgressor may find himself in a situation in which what was once a wished-for advantage has become a burden that can be removed either by paying back the debt or receiving forgiveness . . . Political forgiveness invites the public restoration of the transgressor . . . by publicly releasing the transgressor from debt, the victim is promising not to use the past as the basis for future claims and is inviting others to restore the transgressor's moral position.[13]

Even as churches remain ever culpable for the perpetuation of violence, terror, and injustice against queer people, queer collectives acting as prophets of peace and justice hold the potential for turning the tables and reversing the roles.

Though, while Krisetya argues, prophetic witness to the gospel of peace is the genuine responsibility of religion to the society,[14] a queer reversal of roles means that queer collectives recognizing the subversive potential of forgiveness as a tool for peace and justice take the prophetic mantle upon themselves. The queer enactment of the weak force of forgiveness calls attention to the long history of Christian wrongdoing in relation to LGBTQ lives, extends forgiveness where it is not sought and in the midst of the continued wrongdoing of myriad churches, and vows before an on-looking public that, as queer prophetic witnesses of peace and justice, we invite churches into a more just future in which their transgressions will not forever be held against them.

Experimenting with Forgiveness as Tool for Peace and Justice

As should be clear by now, weak force forgiveness as a subversive tool in the work of peace and justice is a practice far removed from our popular notions of forgiveness. This type of forgiveness cannot be adequately captured with statements like "forgive and forget" or even "forgive them for they know not what they do." Nor can forgiveness as a tool for peace and justice be understood by making forgiveness into an individualistic therapeutic tool, good only for comforting the offended by letting go of the wrongs done to them.

We've been taught a lot of lessons about forgiveness that are utterly unhelpful when it comes to the most insidious forms of evil enacted against us as collectives of people targeted because of an embodiment of human difference. Thus, a little unlearning and relearning may help us to become good experimentalists with forgiveness as a subversive tool for peace and justice. I will offer only four brief suggestions for this experimentation in hopes that collectives of queer people may draw upon their collective wisdom to create more robust and contextualized practices of forgiveness as queer prophets of peace and justice:

1. *Collective, not individual.* The question, "Who can offer such forgiveness?" is an important one. Digeser notes that when an offense like

violence against LGBTQ people focuses on a shared characteristic or identity of a group, the wrong caused by the offense is distributed throughout the group.[15] Thus, the place of forgiveness in the midst of anti-queer violence must be considered by queer people beyond those who become victims of direct physical violence or destruction of property due to their sexual orientation or gender identity. All who share those identifications and are affected by the instrumental nature of these displays of violence must take account of the complex wrongdoing of instrumental violence and the widespread nature of its effects upon queer lives.

When the wrong being perpetrated is toward a collective of people (e.g., religiously-fueled public hatred and denigration of LGBTQ people), acts of forgiveness must also be collective in nature. While many individuals who experience direct physical violence must wrestle with the place of forgiveness in their own lives, when addressing the complexity of instrumental violence, no individual can forgive complex wrongdoing perpetrated against collectives. Likewise, persons outside of the groups being targeted cannot legitimately initiate a process of forgiveness, though they may participate in certain roles when the process is underway. But a collective of people — for example, an LGBTQ religious group or organization — could develop practices that work toward recognition of and accountability for these wrongs through the subversive offering of unsolicited forgiveness.

2. *Enacted, not just felt.* What makes us feel better does not always move us closer toward the realization of a more just world. Weak force forgiveness as a subversive tool for peace and justice is not the therapeutic forgiveness we've grown accustomed to in the literature of popular psychology and self-help religion. It may help us feel good to let go of some wrong done to us or engender a sense of religious piety to take the high road. But that is not the purpose of weak force forgiveness. If forgiveness is to be employed as a tool for peace and justice, it must be enacted rather than simply cathartically felt. Not sentimentalized or therapeutic, the enactment of forgiveness-toward-justice must be coupled with the fortitude to name the wrongs being perpetrated, even when the perpetrators

will not, and bring to light the psychic terror and soul-damaging violence wrapped up in a religiously-fueled climate of anti-queer hatred. These enactments of forgiveness must be vocal and visible.

Without the presence of accountability and the response of repentance on the part of the offender, the process of forgiveness moves beyond sentiment-based conceptions in which forgiveness denotes the removal of resentment, anger, and contempt on the part of the victim.[16] Mesach Krisetya describes what a turn from this sentiment-based process would entail through the language of love, stating, "To love your enemy is to take the other by surprise . . . This kind of love is not emotional but volitional . . . This love is therefore no mere sentimental affection but a positive force for justice and righteousness."[17] While cast in the language of love, Krisetya's analysis is applicable to the process of forgiveness in its subversive movement.

3. *Public, not private.* For collective enactments of forgiveness for unacknowledged wrongdoing to be effective tools in working toward justice, they must be enacted in public. The public nature of this forgiveness serves to call attention to the wrongdoing being perpetrated, even when no one can be brought to account for the damage done and when perpetrators refuse to acknowledge their complicity in the violent denigration of queer lives. This public stand is made without resorting to the same vitriolic, condemnatory tools used by the perpetrators of hate — publicly calling into question both their message and their tools by exemplifying a better way of living together into a future shaped by peace and justice.

4. *Genuine, not feigned.* If forgiveness is practiced as a tool for peace and justice, it must be a forgiveness enacted with the full awareness that repentance and change may never come from religious perpetrators of anti-queer instrumental violence. Yet it is a forgiveness that is enacted in hope for a better, more just future. Some things we've been taught about forgiveness must be unlearned in order to genuinely practice this type of forgiveness. This is not a forgiveness that forgets the wrongdoing being actively perpetrated against the Other. It is not a passive, senti-mentalized forgiveness that is divorced from advocacy and activism. It is

not a forgiveness that makes us feel better about the hatred being leveled against the hated or helps us to let go of our anger over injustice. Instead, it is a forgiveness that faces the realities of hatred and violence and, with a hopeful striving toward justice, publicly enacts forgiveness for those who refuse to acknowledge and cease their wrongdoing. And through that enactment of weak force forgiveness, we express to perpetrators of hatred our commitment to cultivating ways of living into that future together, envisioning a future era of peace even as we continue to resist their acts of violence against us.

5. *Forgiving, not forgetting.* An additional challenge we must overcome in order to enact the weak force of forgiveness is aptly named by theologian Gregory Jones. He notes, "The very notion of 'loving enemies,' tossed off lightly as an injunction, seems to ignore or trivialize the genuine significance of the anger and hostility felt by the people who had been victimized."[18] Rather than ignoring or trivializing the significance of anger, hostility and other emotions of the queer people long subjected to religiously-fueled instrumental violence, the weak force of forgiveness provides a long-sought voice for those feelings to be expressed constructively toward a hoped-for era of peace and justice.

We must leave behind the mentality of forgiving and forgetting and therapeutic forms of forgiveness in order to realize the subversive potential of forgiveness as a tool for peace and justice. It should neither lead to forgetting nor the denial and trivialization of wrongdoing. In this vein, Caputo argues, "Forgiveness is the opposite of repression. In repression, something that is there keeps recurring just because I deny it; in forgiveness, something that is there is dismissed just because I affirm and forgive it."[19]

Digeser adds that perpetrators who deny, cover up, disavow, or evade wrongful acts seek to unburden themselves from their history of offense. Rather than a movement to forget what is in the past through a sentiment-based process of getting over resentment and anger, weak force forgiveness "requires recalling and understanding the past."[20] Forgiveness as a tool for peace and justice must face head on the violent practices of faith communities, knowing that the violence not only assails queer lives, but also diminishes the wellbeing of complicit faith communities even when they deny, cover up, disavow or evade their wrongful acts. It is by no means a willful forgetting, but a vow to remember while working with our offenders toward a more just future wrought by queer people taking up the prophetic mantle of peace too many churches have been unable to bear.

I've struggled with whether what I am describing is really forgiveness or something else entirely. But even amid uncertainty over terminology, I have witnessed the potential of forgiveness to subversively awaken people to the nature of wrongdoing where repeated condemnation often fails.

I once presented a workshop to a group of Christian religious professionals on the radical, subversive potential of forgiveness in the face of violence against LGBTQ people. After I talked for an hour and a half about the violence done to queer people through the anti-queer messages of religious groups, and mused about the potential for acts of forgiveness to bring this wrongdoing to light, one workshop attendee from a denomination that condemns LGBTQ people suddenly seemed to awaken to the point of the workshop. He said in a perturbed tone, "Wait a minute! My church believes homosexuality is a sin and that gay people need God's forgiveness. But it seems like you are saying that we are the ones who need to be forgiven." What could I say? He got it.

After we've addressed the flashy hatred of the most vocal groups like Westboro, we will be left to grapple with the more mundane forms of anti-queer disdain covered by a veneer of tolerance or even love. Beyond Westboro, there remain numerous churches responsible for a history of terror and injustice against queer people — a history for which repentance may never come. Those who have so cruelly called for our repentance, those who thought that forgiveness was theirs to distribute, may now be the ones in need of a queer forgiveness. Perhaps through that subversive queer forgiveness, religious communities intent on maintaining an oppressive and violent status quo will be issued an invitation from an unlikely source into a more just future that they alone could not imagine.

A Constructive Repentance for Churches on the Straight and Narrow

While there are many churches relatively unconcerned with the harm being perpetrated against queer people in their communities, there are also many churches and faith groups exhibiting a desire to enact a process of repentance, seeking forgiveness from the LGBTQ people who have been objects of religiously-fueled denigration and subjected to brutal violence at the hands of Christians.

One such example is a group called "100 Revs" from Sydney, Australia.[21] This group of Christian ministers marched in the world's largest Mardi Gras parade among 10,000 other participants and before a crowd of 300,000. Their march in the parade was an act of contrition enacted before the multitude of queer marchers and onlookers. They sung their way through the parade carrying a sign that read, "Sorry for not acting the way Jesus would have wanted." Many of the churches represented, including Surry Hills Baptist Church, followed this public demonstration of contrite repentance with equally public support for marriage equality in Australia. Their pastor, Mike Hercock, explains the pairing of these actions, saying, "It is one thing for us as ministers to stand up and stand together with our gay brothers and sisters decrying the injustices of the past. It is another to change the future."[22]

In addition to the subversive potential of queer forgiveness, meaningful, public acts of repentance can be enacted by affirming churches wishing to move on to a more just practice of love for queer people. But even churches that haven't quite gotten to the place of theologically affirming same-sex sexuality or gender variance can also cultivate meaningful practices of repentance for the long history of ecclesial destruction of queer lives. Many churches long affirming of LGBTQ people may take steps like those of Surry Hills Baptist Church in Sydney — advocating for marriage equality and the equal treatment of queer people in their community and nation. Still other churches have not resolved their many theological questions in a way that yet allows for this type of public demonstration of full-throated support for justice and equality for LGBTQ persons. Many of these churches do, however, hold a strong desire to do a little better than their predecessors in dialogue on sexual orientation, gender identity, and Christian faith. These congregations wish to exhibit some form of contrition and repentance for the injustice and violence perpetrated against queer people in decades past.

Here, I offer a simple proposal for a constructive repentance for churches in the latter grouping — congregations that have not arrived at a place of full affirmation for LGBTQ persons, but which feel deep regret and a desire to seek forgiveness for the wrongs perpetrated against queer lives under the guise of Christian faithfulness.

First, *a constructive repentance requires us to turn from our suspicious scrutiny and to ask better questions with less potential for harm.* As churches, we have engaged in dialogue on sexuality, gender identity, and faith so poorly for so long — preferring suspicious investigation into human difference, rather than compassionate curiosity — that we must now be willing to stop incessantly repeating our worn our and misguided strategies. This lengthy process of investigation guided by the typical suspicious questions about LGBTQ lives (e.g., "Can one be both queer and a faithful Christian?" "Are same-sex relationships legitimate expressions of covenanted Christian relationship?" etc.) has gone on for so long and with such deleterious effects on LGBTQ lives that to simply say, "We're truly sorry for the damage we've caused and we want to do better in our dialogue on queer lives," is not enough.

When we vocalize this contrition for the way things have gone in the past and iterate a desire for a more hopeful and less violent future, but then return to the dialogue by pursuing the same old questions that have produced so much destruction in the first place we fall short of a true enactment of repentance. We must turn from our old questions and our traditional avenues of suspicious scrutiny of human difference and turn toward more helpful, imaginative, and hopeful questions that exhibit a spirit of compassionate curiosity about queer lives. Even when we have not fully resolved the theological questions about sexuality and gender identity we've asked so persistently in the past, we do know the harm they've caused and must now vow to pursue different lines of inquiry in hopes that these will not only be less likely to lead to violence based upon human difference, but that they may also be more appropriate avenues for theological inquiry and growth.

For example, when we turn to the biblical text for discerning study on the shape of faithful, covenanted relationships, for too long we have asked with incessant narrowness "what the Bible says" about the appropriate gender of one's sexual partner. We have turned to the Bible for clear answers to the trite question, "Is gay okay?" These questions of boundary maintenance — of who is "in" and who is "out" of Christian faithfulness, acceptable intimate relationships, etc. — are the very questions that have led to and supported the construction and maintenance of a theological hierarchy of being and binary divisions of the good and the evil. As described in the previous chapter, the binary thinking that allows for the division of good and evil based upon dichotomies of male/female, straight/gay, etc. and the hierarchical organization of persons according to a theologically-justified view of their value and worth has elicited and validated a long history of instrumental violence against queer bodies that continues to this day.

Churches wishing to enact a process of repentance from this history of violence and degradation of queer people but that cannot yet commit to a biblical/theological position of openness and affirmation of LGBTQ lives might, at very least, commit themselves to a moratorium on the questions of boundary maintenance when approaching the biblical text. For example, a congregation recognizing the violent outcomes these questions have often produced by defining queer people as outside of Christian faithfulness or in positions of inferiority on the theological hierarchies we've constructed may come to experiment with new questions that do not hinge upon the gender of one's intimate, covenanted relationships. Instead, churches may ask more helpful questions seeking to inform the practice of relationship rather than the gendered configuration of relationship.

The questions we might instead ask could include: "When we read the biblical text, what ideals of covenanted relationship emerge as appropriate guides for our teaching about intimate relationship?" "How does our understanding of the gospel influence the way we relate to one another in intimate partnerships?" "How could shifting our attention from the gender of one's significant other to an inquiry into the place of the fruit of the spirit in intimate relationship — love, joy, peace, patience, kindness, generosity, faithfulness, gentleness, self-control (Galatians 5:22-23) — help a greater number of people experience the fullness of abundant life in their most intimate partnerships?" These are no less biblical or faithful questions for churches to ask, but hold far less potential for fueling practices of instrumental violence based upon the embodiment of human difference.

As an aspect of a process of constructive repentance, changing the questions we bring to the biblical text in this way acknowledges that the old questions of boundary maintenance have produced a great deal of violence and marginalization. Thus, rather than say "we're sorry" and continue down the same old paths again and again hoping in vain for a different outcome, we must try new ways of inquiring into the Bible's lessons for the formation of intimate, covenanted relationship.

Second, *a constructive repentance requires us to turn toward actions that demonstrate our contrition.* Repentance requires renewed action. And for churches wishing to genuinely communicate their contrition and enter a process of forgiveness with the queer people who have been objects of disdain and violence fueled by Christian theological messages, more is required than a simple apology. But, unlike the story of Surry Hills Baptist Church above and the many denominations and religious groups working toward equality and justice for LGBTQ lives in the wider public sphere — many churches are not yet able to voice full-throated messages of justice. Some churches are just beginning to clear their throats to even begin a dialogue about sexual orientation and gender identity. But one's current place in the dialogue should not prevent contrite congregations from entering into a process of constructive repentance for the long history of anti-LGBTQ degradation and violence.

For these churches, a simple and very faithful response could go a long way toward placing some meaningful action behind words of deep apology for a history of anti-queer shaming and violence. Recognizing that the many public voices emerging from Christian religious traditions over the past several decades have created havoc and destruction in myriad LGBTQ lives, churches now have the opportunity to intentionally and repentantly shift their public discourse on sexuality. Rather than the sexual moralizing that has shaped much Christian public discourse on LGBTQ lives, churches not yet affirming of queer lives but wishing to enact a process of genuine repentance for Christian-fueled violence may vow, at least temporarily, only to speak publicly about sexual orientation and gender identity when their message is one of anti-violence. This vow might go something like this:

> *Recognizing the long history of Christian voices in fueling a culture of violence against LGBTQ lives, we covenant to practice our repentance for this Christian history by focusing any public voice our community may provide on matters of sexuality and gender identity toward standing on the side of the marginalized to bring an end to the violence so regularly practiced against LGBTQ people. Our continued theological wrestling notwithstanding, we acknowledge our deep belief that all persons are made in the image of God and deserve to live free from the threat of violence. Therefore, as a Christian community, we stand with LGBTQ victims of violence — past, present, and future — seeking to correct a history of Christian irresponsibility*

in both overtly and inadvertently fueling this violence by actively and vocally supporting measures to reduce and eliminate violence against LGBTQ people in our church and community.

Rather than theologizing and moralizing about the legitimacy of queer lives, this stance embodies a commitment to publicly stand on the side of the oppressed, even while all of our theological concerns about same-sex sexuality and gender variance are not yet resolved.

These two commitments — turning away from the suspicious scrutiny that has produced so much destruction and turning toward public practices of anti-violence — are commitments churches across the theological spectrum can make toward repentance for a Christian history of queer marginalization and violence. It can even serve as a starting place for greater public engagement among churches that have already cultivated a space of welcome and affirmation for LGBTQ worshippers.

Theologian Sharon Thornton describes what a future might look like if the response of churches to queer forgiveness is a humble posture of listening. She states, "Listening with imagination means . . . becoming willing to co-imagine a future of restored dignity, freedom, and hope — one in which we are not the chief architects. In this way listening with imagination involves a kind of listening that is not just listening, but *just* listening — a listening that participates in justice."[23]

Churches must recognize that their participation in the process of forgiveness must be divested of ulterior motives, as they are not the chief architects of the newly inaugurated future. Churches must enter this process with queer persons without missionary zeal, not seeking to "win back" the queer people who have needed to leave their faith communities for the sake of their own lives and souls. Joretta Marshall helpfully argues, "Forgiveness is not about trying to fix a relationship; rather it is about honestly facing an injury and hurt that has occurred in the context of some kind of relationship and, in the process, finding ways to move toward justice and liberation."[24] While relational repair may never occur between many churches and the queer people damaged and demeaned by instrumental violence, the process of weak force forgiveness as a tool for peace and justice graciously opens the opportunity for such relational change by inviting churches to shed their past burden of violence in return for a prophetic mantle of peace now demonstrated in the lives of queer people.

Notes

[1] John Swinton, *Raging with Compassion: Pastoral Responses to the Problem of Evil* (Grand Rapids: Eerdmans, 2007), 132. Italics in original text.

[2] This is, of course, not a new question. The question of forgiveness has been astutely addressed in varied contexts of injustice and violence throughout history. A few prime modern examples are Donald B. Kraybill, Steven M. Nolt, and David L. Weaver-Zercher, *Amish Grace: How Forgiveness Transcended Tragedy* (San Francisco: Wiley, 2007); Desmond Tutu, *No Future Without Forgiveness* (New York: Doubleday, 1999); Simon Wiesenthal, *The Sunflower: On the Possibilities and Limits of Forgiveness* (New York: Schocken, 1969/1998). While the reflections in these and other texts are immensely helpful and challenging for faith communities in every era, differences in time and context surrounding any circumstance of grave violence and injustice require that *questions* of forgiveness be revisited and *practices* of forgiveness as a possible tool for peace and justice be continually reshaped and reimagined.

[3] Mesach Krisetya, "Sharing Hope in a Violent World," in *Pastoral Theology's & Pastoral Psychology's Contributions to Helping Heal a Violent World*, ed. G. Michael Cordner (Surakarta, Indonesia: The International Pastoral Care Network for Social Responsibility and DABARA Publishers, 1996), 29.

[4]Karen Lebacqz, *Justice in an Unjust World: Foundations for a Christian Approach to Justice* (Minneapolis: Fortress Press, 1987), 38.

[5]For the Southern Baptist Convention — a denomination formed in the throes of the nation's battle over slavery — it took until *1995* for a robust resolution lamenting the Convention's complicity in the institution of slavery and denouncing practices of racism. The resolution reads in part, "we apologize to all African-Americans for condoning and/or perpetuating individual and systemic racism in our lifetime; and we genuinely repent of racism of which we have been guilty…[and] we ask forgiveness from our African-American brothers and sisters." "Resolution on Racial Reconciliation on the 150th Anniversary of the Southern Baptist Convention," SBC.net: Official Website of the Southern Baptist Convention, accessed April 12, 2013, http://www.sbc.net/resolutions/amresolution.asp?id=899.

[6]John D. Caputo, *The Weakness of God: A Theology of the Event* (Bloomington, IN: Indiana University Press, 2006), 211.

[7]Caputo, *The Weakness of God*, 211-2.

[8]Caputo, *The Weakness of God*, 146.

[9]To capture a part of what Caputo means by weak force it is helpful to make a connection to his conception of the kingdom of God: "The kingdom of God obeys the laws of reversals in virtue of which whatever is first is last, whatever is out is in, whatever is lost is saved, where even death has a certain power over the living, all of which confounds the dynamics of strong forces…The kingdom of God is the rule of weak forces like patience and forgiveness, which, instead of forcibly exacting payment for an offense, release and let go. The kingdom is found whenever war and aggression are met with an offer of peace. The kingdom is a way of living, not in eternity, but in time, a way of living without why, living for the day, like the lilies of the field — figures of weak forces — as opposed to mastering and programming time, calculating the future, containing and managing risk. The kingdom reigns wherever the least and most undesirable are favored while the best and most powerful are put on the defensive." Caputo, *The Weakness of God*, 14-15.

[10]Caputo, *The Weakness of God*, 212.

[11]Caputo, *The Weakness of God*, 213.

[12]Caputo, *The Weakness of God*, 14-15.

[13]P.E. Digeser, *Political Forgiveness* (Ithaca: Cornell University Press, 2001), 87.

[14]Krisetya, "Sharing Hope in a Violent World," 29.

[15]Digeser, *Political Forgiveness*, 112.

[16]Digeser, *Political Forgiveness*, 21-2.

[17]Krisetya, "Sharing Hope in a Violent World," 29.

[18]Gregory L. Jones, *Embodying Forgiveness: A Theological Analysis* (Grand Rapids: Eerdmans, 1995), 242.

[19]Caputo, *The Weakness of God*, 147.

[20]Digeser, *Political Forgiveness*, 3.

[21]Mike Hercock, "100 Revs," in *Rightly Dividing the Word of Truth: A Resource for Congregations in Dialogue on Sexual Orientation and Gender Identity*, 2nd ed., ed. Cody J. Sanders (Charlotte, NC: Baptist Peace Fellowship of North America, 2013), 235-6.

[22]Hercock, "100 Revs," 235.

[23]Sharon, G. Thornton, *Broken Yet Beloved: A Pastoral Theology of the Cross* (St. Louis: Chalice Press, 2002), 201.

[24]Joretta L. Marshall, "Communal Dimensions of Forgiveness: Learning from the Life and Death of Matthew Shepard," *Journal of Pastoral Theology* 9 (1999): 53.

Epilogue

Where Do We Go from Queer?

The Youth Aren't Our Saviors

I regularly participate in conversations in which someone claims, "The next generation doesn't have any problem with queer people. Once the youth of today are the leaders of tomorrow, society will be much more accepting of queer people." Even if this sentiment were accurate, it would still be wrong.

In the first place, the sentiment that "younger generations" are the magical cure to injustice and violence against queer people simply may not be true . . . at all. While there may be something to the notion that greater exposure to LGBTQ people leads to greater tolerance of sexual and gender identity difference, we need only look at the average age of anti-LGBTQ hate crime perpetrators to realize that passive dependence upon younger generations isn't a simple fix to the problems of prejudice and violence we face.

In 2011, the greatest numbers of perpetrators of LGBTQ hate crime violence were between 19-29 years old, comprising 34 percent of all known offenders. Another 13 percent fell between the ages of 15 and 18 years old. Add to that the 2 percent of offenders under the age of 14 and it becomes clear that nearly half (49 percent) of all anti-LGBTQ hate crime offenders are within the age range of persons we often portray as our future saviors from a society marred by anti-queer prejudice and violence. Even more surprisingly, the percentage of offenders in the 19-29 year old range increased 3 percent from the previous year's statistics.[1]

But let's pretend for a moment that it is true that today's youth really are our saviors from a society of prejudice, injustice, and violence toward queer people. Let's just imagine that if we hold on long enough, the youth of today will be the leaders of tomorrow and they'll correct generations of injustice and violence against queer people. Even if things really did pan out this way, it is still the wrong approach for our churches to take toward the work of justice. While today's youth may grow up with greater exposure to LGBTQ figures in the media and in their schools and communities—gradually acclimating them to the existence of queer people in their lives—getting "used to" queer people falls far short of cultivating in their hearts and minds a vision for justice in the face of marginalization and violence.

The simple tolerance that emerges from familiarity with those who differ from us may serve the ends of reducing violence and increasing some modicum of acceptance for difference. But in the struggle to cultivate a social climate characterized by a vision of greater freedom and decreased violence for queer people or any other marginalized group, a *laissez-faire* approach to justice by which we sit and wait for a better time to come falls far short of a gospel imperative to be active workers of justice and intentional provocateurs of peace.

It is also very troublesome that this view subtly denies recognition for the numerous people in "older" generations who have struggled diligently to bring about a climate of greater justice and decreased violence for queer people. Our churches and communities have been gradually shaped and changed toward greater inclusion and justice for queer lives by these faithful witnesses. Many of these persons have had their own hearts and minds changed as their perspectives on queer lives shifted away from prejudice and disdain toward greater affirmation for queer people. Rather than retaining their inherited prejudices, they studied, prayed, and worked—slowly changing the lives, churches, and communities within their influence.

If our posture toward the anticipation of a more just society is one of passive waiting, we have forfeited one of the greatest gifts the struggle for queer rights, inclusion, and justice has to offer—the gift of learning from our past and present circumstances in ways that shape our engagement with concerns of justice into the future. By passively waiting, we fail to learn key lessons about the nature of injustice, marginalization, and violence. We abdicate our responsibility to actively cultivate the minds and hearts of younger generations in devotion to a gospel vision of peace and justice. We must stop waiting. The youth aren't our saviors.

The Work of Justice Has No Final Frontier

Heterosexism—the prejudicial attitudes, institutionalized injustice, and second-class citizenship experienced by queer people—is often called the "last acceptable prejudice" in the United States. Some dedicated activists view the struggle to end heterosexist discrimination "the civil rights movement of our era." It is easy to see why some would see it this way. The public marches and demonstrations for gay rights, the legal battles over unequal distribution of social benefits like marriage and protections like employment nondiscrimination for queer people, the dehumanizing rhetoric employed by those who decry the impending demise of civilization if queer people are given equal footing with heterosexuals—all of this looks rather similar to the civil rights struggles of our past. And, to many, all of this does seem like "*the* civil rights movement of our era" over "*the* last acceptable prejudice" in the United States.

But with deep respect for my queer colleagues in the work of justice and the myriad churches and organizations espousing these views, I must disagree wholeheartedly. In our long striving toward justice, there is no final frontier.

For many—especially for able-bodied, white, middle- and upper-class gay and bisexual men in the United States—the experience of prejudice, injustice, and violence based upon sexual orientation has been the first personal experience of systemic injustice in our lives. We have never experienced the dehumanizing mechanisms of racism, the social structures of gender inequality, arrangements of physical space that do not take our bodies into account, or the systemic constraints of classism. For many who find themselves disadvantaged by the law[2] and subject to prejudice and violence from friends and neighbors but who have very little personal experience of injustice or marginalization in other regards, gay rights can really seem like the civil rights movement of our era over the last acceptable prejudice. If we could just get this injustice righted, we'd be solidly on track in church and society.

But this is far from the truth. My persistent fear is that with the increase of rights, inclusion, and protections for queer people, many who have dedicated their time, energy, and funding to achieve these progressive gains toward justice will gradually sense their fervor for the work of justice wane. If we engage in the work of justice-seeking under the "last prejudice" myth, we might rest satisfied when our struggle for LGBTQ rights and inclusion is resolved. This is a terrifying prospect.

We must rid ourselves of the myth that heterosexism is the last acceptable prejudice and the pinnacle of civil rights striving in our era. Likewise, we can no longer afford to operate by a silo approach to justice—working upon one group's circumstances of injustice and marginalization apart from all others. In order to more fully engage our calling to the work of justice, we must develop a more robust understanding of the interconnected nature of oppressions—sexism, racism, classism, ableism, heterosexism, etc.—all connected within a system of injustice and violence that makes each iteration of oppression possible. While we should remain pastorally attentive to the particularities of each unique human experience of suffering due to injustice and violence, we must conceptually widen our view to allow for more effective strategies in the work of justice.

We don't have to look far in order to rupture the myth that heterosexism is the pinnacle rights issue of our day. Whether the increasing prejudicial attitudes towards Muslims in an era of religious plurality, the vitriol spewed in public discussions over how a nation will treat its many immigrants, the ever widening wealth gap between the extraordinary rich and the devastatingly poor, or the racial bias represented in our legal system and prisons, it is clear that justice has no final frontier. The struggle for LGBTQ rights is but one of an expanding catalogue of concerns calling for the pastoral attention and the prophetic action of communities of faith.

Many who cut their activist teeth in the black civil rights movement of the 1950s-60s brought their strategies and perspectives on justice into the gay rights movement of the 1960s-70s. Many individuals and churches should now be asking, "For those of us who have cut our activist teeth in movements for queer rights, inclusion, and justice, how can we apply what we have learned to prophetically engage other concerns of justice?" We cannot let the embers that burn in our hearts for justice grow dim when our particular concerns are resolved and our pet projects finally bring about success in the struggle for queer rights and inclusion. The work of justice has no final frontier.

Notes

[1] The National Coalition of Anti-Violence Programs, *Hate Violence Against Lesbian, Gay, Bisexual, Transgender, Queer, and HIV-affected Communities in the United States in 2011* (New York: New York City Gay & Lesbian Anti-Violence Project, Inc., 2012), accessed January 25, 2013, http://www.avp.org/storage/documents/Reports/2012_NCAVP_2011_HV_Report.pdf.

[2] Not only is this legally disadvantaged status noticeable in the very prominent concerns we've become accustomed to addressing in the public square about same-sex marriage equality, but it is also felt in the workplace inequality experienced by LGBT people. For example, at the time of this writing, it is perfectly legal in 29 states for a person to be fired or denied a job because of a lesbian, gay, bisexual identification and it is legal in 34 states to discriminate in the workplace based upon one's transgender identification. See "Statewide Employment Laws & Policies," *Human Rights Campaign*

(Washington, DC: Human Rights Campaign), accessed April 1, 2013, http://www.hrc.
org/files/assets/resources/Employment_Laws_and_Policies.pdf.